STRESS OF STUDENT TEACHERS

STRESS OF STUDENT TEACHERS

By

Timmisetti Brahmaiah

M.Sc., M.Ed.

Lecturer, College of Education

Guntur, Andhra Pradesh

Editor

Dr. Digumarti Bhaskara Rao

M.Sc., M.A., M.A., M.Ed., Ph.D.

Reader & Research Director

R.V.R. College of Education

Guntur – 522006, A.P.

digumartibhaskararao@rediffmail.com

DISCOVERY PUBLISHING HOUSE PVT. LTD.

NEW DELHI-110 002

First Published-2009
Reprinted: 2013
ISBN 978-81-8356-376-5

Published by:

DISCOVERY PUBLISHING HOUSE PVT. LTD.
4831/24, Ansari Road, Prahlad Street
Darya Ganj, New Delhi-110002 (India)
Phone: 23279245 • Fax: 91-11-23253475
E-mail: dphbooks@rediffmail.com
dphtemp@indiatimes.com
web: www.discoverypublishinghouse.com

Printed at:

Dynamic printers, Delhi

Dedicated

to

Mr. Koneru Suresh Babu

Mrs. Koneru Vijaya Lakshmi

Siddartha Group of Educational Institutions

Eluru, West Godavari, AP

in appreciation of their
service to education

PREFACE

Stress is inevitable in any educational institution. In optimal limits, it mobilises the potentialities of the students to perform more effectively. However, increasing amount of academic stress for prolonged periods may create stress in the students which may affect their mental health, study habits and academic achievement.

Failure in examination, underachievement and the resulting stress are becoming prominent features of educational life at school as well as the higher educational levels, leading to a wide range of health problems having far-reaching consequences for individual as well as societal well being.

Under these circumstances, a study has been undertaken to study the stress of student teachers pursuing B.Ed. course in Colleges of Education. Except locality, the gender, the methodology of teaching, and the qualification of student teachers did show their influence on the level of stress of student teachers. The female student teachers, the science methodology student teachers and the graduate student teachers had more stress than their counterparts.

The student teachers should learn to recognise the warnings signs of stress, intervene to calm themselves down physically, modify their thoughts in a way that reduce their frustration, fix goals as per their abilities and necessities, learn to communicate assertively, and dare to ask for help in order to prevent stress.

This study would be of great use to teacher educators and educational planners and administrators in solving out the problems related to stress and in developing a teacher education curriculum which does not develop stress among the student teachers.

Dr. Digumarti Bhaskara Rao

Sri Sai Soudha
D-43, S.V.N. Colony
Guntur 522006
A.P., India

CONTENTS

1

INTRODUCTION

"Stress is like an electric power. It can make a bulb light up and provide brilliant illumination. However, if the voltage is higher than what the bulb can take, it can burn out the bulb." *(H. Mahadevan)*

Stress has become an inevitable part of human life. It is an emotional, intellectual and/or physical response to an internal and/or external change, demand and/or pressure. The causes for it are many and multidimensional those include environmental, physiological, social or personal thoughts, hassles, pressures, frustrations, conflicts, failures, sorrows, selfishness, greed, carrying, hurt feelings, comparisons, competitions, victimisations and/or fear. Any change, challenge or thereat that exceeds the coping abilities of an individual is known as stress.

Stress, at the Stress Management Conference (1989), was defined as:

Stress = high demands + high constraints +low support.

Stress is the physiological, psychological, and behavioural response of an individual to both external and internal pressures. These pressures are known as stressors. Our ability to recognize and deal with stress effectively has become one of the most pressing needs of our age even among the school going and college students.

In our life, stress is daily experience. Stress is an unavoidable consequence. The only stressless state is death. Stress implies pressure, tension of worry, resulting in problems in all walks of life. Life without stress would be no life at all. All change is stressful, but when it exceeds one's limit it needs to be considered.

Stress is inevitable in any educational institution. In optimal limits, it mobilises the potentialities of the students to perform more effectively. However, increasing amount of academic stress for prolonged periods may create frustration in the students which may affect their mental health, study habits and academic achievement.

Stress has been defined as "the state manifested by the specific syndrome, which consists of all the non-specific induced changes within a biological system" (Selye, 1974). Stress is usually thought of in negative terms like causing something bad or distress to the individual. But, there is also a positive and pleasant side of stress, leading to good things. It can be defined as an adoptive response to a situation resulting in physical and psychological and behavioural deviations. Stress is not simply anxiety or nervous tension and necessarily something damaging or bad, which needs to be avoided. Stress is inevitable at sometime or other. But, it can be prevented or can effectively be controlled to some extent if proper measures are taken depending on the nature of factors and their affects on stress.

It's an open secret that life at competitive institutions, especially professional colleges, is highly stressful. Rigorous course work and higher congested schedules coupled with fears of failure because students feel stressed at same point in their college careers. The demands and pressures of parents and high aspirations can be a source of stress for students. Pessimistic thoughts and unhappy feelings can also generate stress and contribute to its symptoms. Stress is an adaptive mechanism, through which the body, attempts to protect itself in threatening situations. A certain amount of stress is necessary in daily life; in fact, we must experience some minor degree of stress just to get going in the morning. Some studies suggest that up to a point stress can improve performance, and so is actually a good thing. Beyond that point, however, stress only makes things worse.

Stress among the school going, college and professional students is the burning issue these days. It has become a serious threat disturbing physical and mental health and harmonious relations with the members of the family and the people outside, at study or workplace.

Adolescence is the period of considerable stress. While much of the stress can be minimised through support, persistence, active decision making and planning, there still will be times when adolescents find themselves in different situations. Coping with the stress is associated with various competencies such as organisational adaptability, human relations, problem solving and self confidence.

The educational system, in practice as such is laying too much emphasis on examinations, marks, ranks and degrees than developing productive and good human beings. The institutional efforts are to turn out more careerists than bringing about excellence of spirit. The teachers strive for academic excellence but do not facilitate learners to flower as total human beings. Parents resort to comparative evaluation of their children rather than to nourish their sensibility and sensitivity. The society encourages the demands of job and earning first but not their ability to deal with complex ways of daily living.

STATEMENT OF THE PROBLEM

A Study of Stress of Student Teachers.

NEED OF THE STUDY

Health problems may arise due to incompatibility between the demands of the educational system and the characteristics of learner or between learner's expectations and the educational processes or both. Such incompatibilities are becoming more and salient in the context of increasing competition in the job market, increased pressure for achievement from parents, uncertain future and parental aspirations and their desire for compensation through their progeny.

Failure in examination, underachievement and the resulting frustration are becoming prominent features of educational life at school as well as at the higher educational levels, leading to a wide range of health problems having far reaching consequences for individual as well as societal well being. This is reflected in a recent analysis of suicide among students. Since the cause which they are studying is only one year but the syllabus and the project works to be completed are many, the Student teachers are facing more stress in completing their project work in time.

So, teacher educators, administrators, policy planners and guidance personnel connected with teacher education programmes should think of ways and means of reducing the level of stress among the student teacher so that they can perform still better to improve the qualities among their students when they join the schools.

SCOPE OF THE STUDY

The present study is confined to the Guntur district. The sample selected for the study was student teachers, who were studying in the Colleges of Education and the sample size chosen for the present study was 310 (three hundred and ten) student teachers only.

The variables chosen for the study were gender (male and female), locality (rural and urban), teaching methodology (arts and science) of Student teachers, and educational qualification (graduation and post-graduation).

The other factors that are contributing to the present study are socio-economic status, home background of the students, age, creativity, achievement, personality, birth order, intelligence, adjustment, attitudes, (parents as well as students), motivation, etc., are not taken because of time and money. The researcher has confined the study to four variables only namely, gender, locality, methodology of study and educational gratification of the student teachers.

OBJECTIVES OF THE STUDY

The objectives of the study were:

1. To find out the stress of student teachers;
2. To find out the stress of male and female student teachers;

3. To find out the stress of rural and urban student teachers;
4. To find out the stress of arts and science teaching methodology of student teachers;
5. To find out the stress of graduate and postgraduate student teachers.

EDUCATIONAL IMPLICATIONS OF THE STUDY

The present study will help the people and personnel involved in teacher education in reducing the stress of student teachers if found it in them. It also helps in devising suitable strategies and programmes either to avoid or to reduce stress. If stress avoiding and reducing strategies and programmes are informed to student teachers, they will implement them in classrooms when they become teachers.

2

REVIEW OF RELATED LITERATURE

Any worthwhile research study in any field of knowledge requires an adequate familiarity with the work which has already been done in the same area. A summary of writings of recognised authorities and of previous research provides evidence that the researcher is familiar with what is already known and what is still unknown and untested. Since affective research is based upon past knowledge, this step helps to eliminate the duplication of what has been done, and provides useful hypotheses and helpful suggestions for significant investigation.

Citing studies that show substantial agreement and those that seem to present conflicting conclusions helps to sharpen and define understanding of existing knowledge in the problem area provides a background for the research project and makes the researcher aware of the status of the issue. Parading a long list of annotated studies relating to the problem is ineffective and inappropriate. Only those studies that are plainly relevant, competently executed and reported should be included (Bhaskara Rao, D., 1997)

Capitalising on the review of expert researchers can be fruitful in providing helpful ideas and suggestions. While review articles that summarise related studies are useful, they do not provide a satisfactory substitute for an independent research. Even though the review of related literature is not a substitute for an independent work, it is one of the first steps in the research process. It is a valuable guide to define the problem, to recognise its significance, to suggest promising data gathering devices, to appropriate the study design and the sources of data for affective analysis and to arrive at fruitful conclusions. (B.V. Kumari and D. Bhaskara Rao, 2000)

The search for related literature is a time consuming process, even though it is necessary, as earlier stated, for a good research work. Hence, this chapter on review of related literature is meant for the study of literature rated to the stress.

THEORETICAL PERSPECTIVES

The term 'stress' was first coined in 1822 by the French Mathematician Augustine Cauchy. He defined stress as a pressure per unit area.

In the twentieth century, stress concept entered the field of Biological Sciences. Walter Cannon (1914) conducted psychological research which resulted in his describing the stress response as a 'fight' or 'flight' response.

Hons Selye (1936), a Canadian Endocrinologist, continued this work and devised the general adaptation syndrome, a model of how the body responds to stressful situations in the short and long term. He began the trend to describe pressures with the term 'stressors' and the biological response as "stress". He defined biological stress as the sum of non-specific changes in the body caused by functions or damage. Physical scientists use 'stress' to indicate a force pressure or stimulus, whereas biological scientists and psychologists use 'stress' to indicate a change or response.

The word 'stress' is used in psychology in two different ways. It is defined as a state of psychological upset or disqualification in the human beings caused by frustration, conflict and other internal and external strains and pressures. In more serious condition of stress, the individual's physical processes are seriously affected. The mental processes are confused and the emotional state is chaotic. The stress is regarded as a class of stimuli which threaten an individual in some way and this causes disturbances in his behaviour.

Meaning of Stress

Stress can be defined in a number of different ways to understand its meaning.

Stress is seen as characteristic of the environment, for example, work-related stresses, life events such as bereavement, daily hassles, etc.

Stress is seen as a person's response to the characteristics of the environment. This is based on Selye's ideas. Any stimulus which produces the stress response is a stressor.

A process of behavioural, emotional, mental and physical reactions, caused by prolonged, increasing or new pressures which are significantly greater than coping resources is stress. (Dunham, 1984)

Stress is any unpleasant and disturbing emotional experience due to frustration. (Scott, 1988)

Stress is the affect on a person of being subjected to serious stimulation or the threat of such stimulation particularly when he/she is unable to avoid or terminate the conditions. (Stratton and Hayes, 1988)

Stress is a process of appraising events or threatening, challenging, or harmful and responding to such events on a physiological, emotional, cognitive, or behavioural level. (Robert S. Feldman, 1989)

Stress is a state of tension produced by pressure or conflicting demands with which the person cannot adequately cope. (Jary and Jary, 1995)

The discomfort people are feeling is stress. (Keenan,1998)

Stress is the "wear and tear" that our minds and bodies experience as we attempt to cope with our continually changing environment. (Geddes and Grosset, 1996)

Stress is an excess of demands over the individual's ability to meet them. (Atkinson, 1999)

The term 'a state of stress' to denote a specific syndrome occurring in the body in response to certain agents to which he refers to is as "stressors". (Hans Selye, 1976)

Stress, like a motive, may be partly or wholly unconscious, through the presence of uneasiness or anxiety may be the clue that stress is present. Stress is inevitable and sometimes chosen voluntarily. Mental health results not from lack of stress but ability to cope with it satisfactorily. (Coleman)

A convenient definition of stress is any stimulus or change in the external or internal environment which disturbs homeostasis which, under certain conditions, can result in illness.

Stress: Past and Present

Stress is present in all societies. Whenever man interacts with other people and the environment, certain amount of stress is created.

Stress is, in fact, as old as the history of mankind. It is a biochemical and behavioural reaction which has its origin in the 'fight or flight' response, an expression of the instinct of conservation which can be traced to the primitive caveman.

But, today, man is seldom faced with the need for fight or flight as most of the threats we experience are not physical threats requiring quick action.

Sources of Stress

A. Psycho-social sources

B. Physiological sources.

A. Psycho-social Sources

(i) ***Adaptation:*** Every time we are confronted with change, either the event is desirable or undesirable, the homeostasis is disrupted or we undergo stress during the period of adaptation to the event. The magnitude of experienced stress is dependent on two factors: (1) The intensity and frequency of change, and (2) Our power of adaptability.

(ii) ***Frustration:*** Emotionally, we respond to frustration with feelings of anger, despair and aggression, whether exteriorised or interiorized.

(iii) *Overload*: The four main factors which contribute to the excessive demands are: (1) Time pressures; (2) Excessive responsibility; (3) Lack of support; and (4) Excessive expectations from ourselves and from those around us.

(iv) *Self-Perception*: Individuals who have a low level of self-esteem and assurance are considerably more prone to negative attitudes than those who hold a confident and positive image of themselves.

(v) *Behaviour*: The way we generally interact with the environment can prediscope us to stress and related diseases.

(vi) *Anxiety*: Anxious reactive persons are prone to high levels of stress through a feedback system. People who are hypersensitive to stressful reactions due to anxiety tend to: (1) worry unnecessarily; (2) catastrophize; (3) relieve unpleasant events of the past, and (4) have a pessimistic view of life.

(vii) *Lack of Control*: One of the most powerful stressors of all is the real or imagined loss of control, especially in the individuals who have a strong need to control themselves and their environment.

B. *Physiological Sources*

(i) *Nutrition*: Inadequate dietary habits can contribute to or cause stress. The consumption of certain foods, e.g. coffee, tea, cola beverages, etc.

(ii) *Over-eating and Under-eating*: High intake of food results in obesity which in turn can lead to ill health and a variety of diseases. Likewise, taking in too few calories or eating an unbalanced diet lowers our resistance to stress.

(iii) *Vitamin Deficiency*: During stressful times, higher intake of certain vitamins is needed to maintain the nervous and endocrine systems. They are: Vitamin C and Vitamin of the B complex, particularly B1, B2, B5, B6.

(iv) *Smoking*: Tobacco contains nicotine. Like caffeine, it is a sympathomimetic agent which triggers the stress response, i.e., stimulates the adrenal glands, releasing hormones which elicit the stress response.

(v) *Noise*: Noise can cause stress by stimulating the sympathetic nervous system, by causing irritation and by decreasing concentration power.

(vi) *Techno Stress*: Initially, it was thought that technology would cut work time in half and that there would be more spare time to enjoy. Instead, the work load has become dense, deadlines more compressed, expectations higher, together with less human contact and communication.

Symptoms of Stress

Some of the examples of symptoms of stress are:

- Cardiovascular disease
- Obesity
- Diabetes
- Skin disorder
- Ulcers
- Alcohol abuse
- Tobacco abuse
- Insomnia
- Backaches and headaches
- Sexual problems
- Mental and physical fatigue
- Muscle tension

Sites of Stress Symptoms

The stress reaction and its affect involve the brain and all our bodily functions Stress ultimately affects our

- Perceptual senses
- Nervous system

- Hormonal balance
- Cardiovascular system
- Digestive system
- Skin
- Urogenital tracts
- Immune system

Factors Determining Severity of Stress

(A) The Intensity of Stress

(B) Stress Tolerance capacity

A. The Intensity of Stress

It is an intensity of the stress that makes severe and it depends on the following factors:

(i) ***Duration of Stress***: The length of a stress may turn it into a mild or severe stress;

(ii) ***Number of Stresses***: Facing a number of stresses at the same time will result in a more severe situation than if these stresses are suffered separately;

(iii) ***Amount of Anticipated Stress***: How much the individual suffers as a result of the stress situation if these are not met in a positive way depends on the degree of anticipation which may increase or decrease the severity of stress;

(iv) ***Strength and Quality of the Sources of Stress***: The nature of the stress will also depend upon the strength and quality of frustration, conflicts, pressures or other stimuli originating from the stress events.

B. Stress Tolerance Capacity

It has been observed that people are able to weather severe adverse circumstances without showing significant psychological damage. They are able to handle the most threatening situations without much difficulty while others breakdown under relatively mild stress. The term stress tolerance thus refers to the amount of stress one can tolerate before breaking down under the pressure of stress.

Stages of Stress

- *The Alarm Reaction–Positive Phase*: A certain amount of stress or stimulation is essential to our health and performance. This is the positive phase of stress.
- *Adaptation or Resistance–Negative Phase*: Where stress continues to increase 'distress' begins, health and performance decrease. This corresponds to the negative phase of stress.

Once we pass the peak of our stress curve, both health and performance decline.

Recognition of Stress

We all have different threshold to stress, and the kinetics at the curve, differ from one individual to another depending on bodily bio-chemical makeup.

Phase 1—Positive phase of stress results in:

- Enthusiasm
- Optimism
- Positive outlook
- Physical stamina
- Mental alertness
- Optimal personal relationships
- High productivity and creativity.

Phase 2—Negative phase of stress prone to :

- Fatigue
- Irritability
- Lack of concentration
- Depression
- Pessimism

- Illness
- Low productivity and low creativity.

Stress Arousal

Two broad types of adjustment to stress have been identified. They are situational and transitional adjustments.

- ***Situational Adjustment***

Situational adjustment is required in order to deal with demands due to environmental circumstances. The sudden illness of a loved one, a natural disaster and war are special events that require adjustment.

Examples of everyday situations that often produce stress reactions include taking a test and entering a new social setting. In fact, stress reactions to these activities are so common that we have special names for them.

There are several ways of responding to the stress or being evaluated. The most adaptive response is active, specific and direct.

- ***Transitional Adjustment***

It is a normal part of human development. While transitional changes occur more gradually than situational one do. The need for transitional adjustment may see sudden for the person going through of. Some of the transitions in the life cycle that people respond to with varying degree of stress include birth and establishing a good relationship between mother and baby. Initial steps towards independence, the biological and social change of adolescence, are major educational transitions such as going to college, entry into the world of work, marriage, having children and child rearing.

Coping with Stress

People can deal with different ways. Getting on with the problem at hand is usually the best adaptive approach and is most likely to occur when the individual is not hampered by vulnerabilities. Anxiety, defensiveness and anger are more likely to occur in vulnerable individuals. People who cope effectively with stressful situations have first learned to direct their thoughts along productive lines and to avoid being distracted by fear and worry. Coping with stress involves learning how to think constructively, to solve problems, to behave flexible and to provide oneself with feedback about which tactic work and which do not.

Ways of Dealing with Stress

		Task-oriented response
		(Person has resources to cope)
Situation	Stress	Anxiety (Person does not have coping resources)
		Defensive response
		Anger (Person blames the situation)

Stress Management/Relaxation Techniques

- Deep breathing
- Meditation
- Yoga
- Aroma therapy

Breathing is an involuntary, automatic function which reflects our general state of stress arousal, but is at the same time voluntary and can be controlled. Therefore, constant, steady, restful breathing promotes relaxation.

Stress is a fact of life. It is all round us, at work, in our environment and in our personal lives. Because stress arises from so many different factors and conditions, it's probably impossible to eliminate it completely. But, we can apply techniques to lessen its potentially harmful effects (Carver, Scheier and Weintraub, 1989; Folkman, et. al., 1986). Let's consider these techniques, dividing them into three major categories: Physiological, Cognitive and Behavioural.

- ***Physiological Coping Techniques***

Common physiological responses to stress include tense muscles, racing pulse, pounding brut, dry mouth and sweating. But several coping techniques can be affective.

One of the most effective procedures is learning to reduce the tension in our own muscles through progressive relaxation (Jacobson, 1939). To use the technique, begin by alternately flexing and relaxing your muscles to appreciate the difference between relaxed and tense muscles. Next you might shake out you arms and then let them flop by your sides. Then relax your shoulders by slowly rolling them up and down. Now relax your neck, step by step, you extend this process until your body is completely relaxed from head to toe. Controlled breathing is also important.

A relaxed technique that is often effective for achieving a relaxed state is meditation.

Vigorous physical exercise is another important technique for coping with stress.

- ***Behaviour Coping Techniques***

We are all guilty of behaving in ways that stress on ourselves. We overload our schedules with too many responsibilities, we procrastinate, it all adds up to stress. There are plenty of things we can do to reduce the stress in our lives.

One method is time management: learning how to make time work for us instead of against us.

- ***Cognitive Coping Techniques***

We do not always have control over all the stressors in our lives. We can, however, gain some control over our cognitive reactions to them. In other words, when exposed to a stressful situation, we can think about it in different ways, and some of these are much more beneficial than others.

The process of replacing negative appraisal of stressors with more positive ones is called cognitive restructuring (Meichen Baum, 1977). To use this technique successfully, begin by monitoring what you say to yourself during periods of stress.

RESEARCH STUDIES

The following are findings of some of the related research studies:

Stress and Gender

Aggarwal, M. (1985) found that stress scores were higher in case of males when compared to females among university students.

Albuguergue (1987) noticed a significant difference in stress among male and female students.

Bisht, A.R. (1980) found that school climate and academic stress did not differ sex-wise among school going children.

Gouri Prasad, P. (2005) observed a difference in stress of men and women teachers, but not significant. The women teachers have more stress than men teachers, because of lack of good relationship and lack of separate staff rooms for lady teachers.

Gupta (1979) reported that psychological stress was observed to be independent at affect of sex.

Jaiprakash and Bhogle (1994) found that there is no significant difference between male and female under-graduate students in relation to stress. Stress is independent of sex.

Jones (1993) reported that stress is independent of sex, i.e., there is a significant difference between male and female students.

Nageswara Rao, U. (2007) reported that there is no significant difference between male and female teachers working in different high schools of Vizianagaram district in possession of stress towards teaching profession.

Narayana and Ramachandra Reddy (1998) found that there is a significant difference in stress among male and female Intermediate students and also their achievement.

Naidu and Thapa (1978) noticed a significant difference in stress among female and male graduate students.

Padmasri, J.V (1992) reported that stress among boys and girls differed significantly, boys being higher in stress.

Raju, Ramana and Jyothi (2004) noticed that stress has a significant affect on males and females in their achievement of Mathematics.

Ranganathan, Namita (1988) found that boys were found to have higher degree of stress than girls among school-going children.

Shanti Pramod (1998) reported that stress has relation to sex of the students and it also affects in their achievement.

Shrivastava (1981) found that high competence subjects perceived less stress than the low competence subjects among physically handicapped children.

Singh, A.S. and N. Rao (1977) identified that female teachers had greater general perceived stress (G.P.S.) than male counterparts.

Verma and Supriya (1995) found that stress is independent of gender among post-graduate students of Chandigarh University.

Vijaya Lakshmi, G. and Lavanya, P. (2006) observed that male students have more amount of stress than female intermediate students.

Wagner and Compas (1990) reported that stress is independent of sex among post-graduate students.

- **Stress and Locality**

Agarwal, M. (1985) found that stress scores were higher in case of rural students when compared to urban students among University students.

Gouri Prasad, P. (2005) found a difference in stress between urban and rural school teachers, but not significant. The urban school teachers have more stress than rural school teachers, because of higher level of monitoring and problems and extra classes.

Gupta (1970) reported that there is a highly significant difference between the rural and urban students on psychological stress.

Ranganathan, Namita (1988) observed that children in government run schools were found to have higher degree of stress than private schools among school children.

Nageswara Rao, U. (2007) found that there is no significant difference between teachers working in rural and urban localities in Vizianagaram district in possession of stress towards teaching profession.

- **Stress and Subjects**

Agarwal, M. (1985) reported that stress scores were higher in case of science students than arts students among University students.

Gupta (1979) found that students offering science and arts as their academic streams did not differ significantly on any measures of psychological stress.

Prasad Babu, B. and Nageswara Rao, S. (2006) found that the amount of academic stress among adolescents of science stream was higher as compared to arts students; probably because they have to be more punctual in attending the classes and to bear other burdens.

- **Stress and Educational Qualifications**

Gupta (1979) found that students studying in post-graduate classes significantly outscored the students in Grade XI on all measures of psychological stress.

Nageswara Rao, U. (2007) noticed no significant between graduate teachers and post graduate teachers working in different high schools of Vizianagaram district in possession stress towards teaching profession.

Ranganathan, Namita (1988) found that standard in which child studying was not found to influence stress among school children.

Vijaya Lakshmi, G. and Lavanya, P. (2006) reported that Senior Intermediate students have more amount of stress than Junior Intermediate students.

Viswanatha Reddy, P. and Srikanth Reddy, V. (2004) found that children at primary level experienced more stress than high school children in educational and social areas and also reported that coping is used more by high school children than children of primary school.

- **Stress and Academic Achievement**

Bisht, A.R. (1980) found that need for academic achievement was a significant predictor of institutional stress and academic stress even when the need for academic achievement's correlated variance with other variables was partially out.

Padmasri, J.V. (1992) reported that stress yield to be significant correlation with academic achievement among school children.

Ranganathan, Namitha (1988) found that stress was negatively related to academic performance among school children.

- **Stress and Climate**

Bisht, A.R (1980) reported that school climate and academic stress did not differ significantly.

Ranganathan, Namita (1988) found that stress was positively and significantly correlated with the organisational climate in schools among school-going children.

3

RESEARCH DESIGN

Research is a systematic enquiry seeking facts through objective verifiable methods in order to discover the relationship among them and to deduce from them the broad principles or laws. Therefore, the very success of a research work depends upon collecting the necessary information. Several methods of collecting information are developed to assist the research. Every survey expert has his own ideas of selecting the best method of collecting information as it can not be uniform to all. Selection of the method depends on the type of information to be gathered and sources of information to be consulted. For the present study, normative survey method is chosen.

Survey means viewing and interpreting things rigorously and comprehensively. Now-a-days, survey method is a popular way of collecting data and analysing the results statistically and systematically. This method is suitable to this study as this one is a status study.

OPERATIONAL DEFINITIONS OF KEY TERMS

The operational definitions of the important key terms used in the present study on "A Study of Stress of Student teachers" are discussed and defined herewith:

Study

Study refers to a systematic investigation which is objective and research-oriented.

Student Teachers

Student teachers studying in Colleges of Education.

Stress

Stress is any stimulus or change in the external or internal environment which disturbs homeostasis which under certain conditions can result in illness.

Gender

Gender refers to male and female student teaches.

Locality

Locality refers to rural and urban areas.

Methodology

Methodology refers to the method of study under which the student has been admitted into the course. For the present study, Arts and science teaching methodologies were considered.

- *Arts methodology*: Where the student studies 'Methodology of teaching Social Studies' as the elective subject.
- *Science methodology*: Where the student studies Methodology of Teaching Biological Science or Physical Science' as the elective subject.

Educational Qualifications

Educational qualification refers to whether the student is a graduate or a post-graduate. For the present study, arts graduates and post-graduates and science graduates and post-graduates were considered.

- *Graduates*: Those who have completed their three years degree course of study in arts or science or commerce as a specialised subject.

- *Postgraduates*: Those who have completed their two years post graduate course of study in arts or science or commerce as a specialised subject.

VARIABLES OF THE STUDY

Variables are the conditions or characteristics that the experimenter manipulates, controls and observes. There are mainly three types of variables, namely, independent, dependent and intervening. The independent variables are those variables which do not change on manipulation by the experimenter. The dependent variables are those variables which change on manipulation done by the experimenter. The intervening variables are those variables which are dependent both on dependent and independent variables.

For the present study, the following independent variables are chosen:

Gender

Male and female student teachers;

Locality

Rural and urban student teachers;

Methodology

Arts and Science teaching methodology student teachers.

Educational Qualification

Graduate and post-graduate student teachers.

HYPOTHESES OF THE STUDY

Hypothesis is a tentative generalisation which provides basis to the whole study to be tested by facts. It is a shrewd and intelligent guess, supposition, inference, hunch, provisional statement, a tentative generalisation to the existence of some fact, condition or relationship relative to some phenomena which serves to explain already known facts in a given area of knowledge and which guides the search for new truth on the basis of empirical evidence.

In statistical hypothesis, the sample should be representative of the whole population. This can be ensured in random sampling where the units of population have got equal chances of being represented. The hypothesis to be tested in this study is "null hypothesis". Ordinarily, a null hypothesis is a statement to believe that there is no relation to the independent and dependent variable. Once it is formulated, depending on the outcome, it will be either accepted or rejected.

For the present study the following hypotheses were framed:

- There is no stress in Student teachers;
- There is no significant difference in the stress of male and female student teachers;
- There is no significant difference in the stress of rural and urban student teachers;
- There is no significant difference in stress of arts and science teaching methodology student teachers;
- There is no significant difference in the stress of graduate and postgraduate student teachers.

SAMPLE OF THE STUDY

A sample is a smaller representation of the larger whole. A sample contains primarily sampling units and a slice of the population representing the universe. A sample must possess the essential characteristics such as representativeness, adequacy, homogeneity, lack at bias, smallness in size, accuracy and completeness to yield accurate results.

Sampling is the easiest method of social investigation. The purpose of the sampling is to draw inferences concerning the universe. There are three elements in the process of sampling. They are selection of sample, collection of information and drawing inferences. According to Cornell, "Sampling is the process by which a relatively small number of individuals are selected or analysed in order to find out something about the entire population or the universe from which it is selected".

In any research, various methods are utilised for selection of sample. After a detailed study of all the methods, the stratified random sampling method was selected for the present study. Stratified random sampling assures each individual element in the universe as equal chance of being chosen. This is suitable for the present study as the universe considered for the study is homogenous.

In order to reduce sampling error a sample of 310 student teachers was chosen. In this study, the strata divided are represented in the following table:

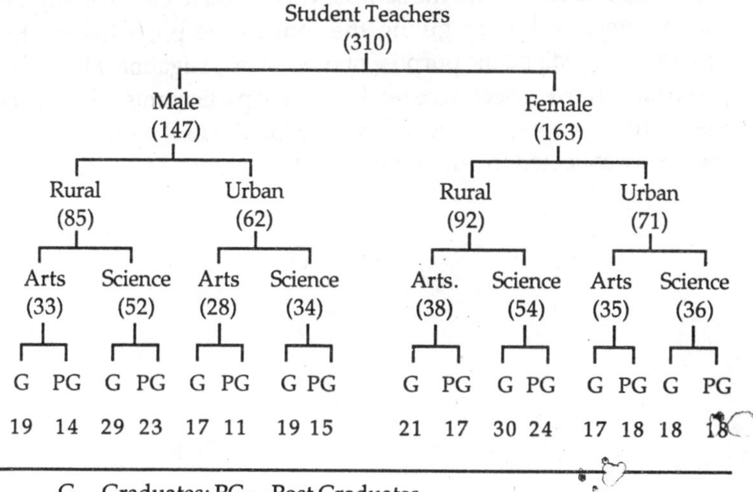

G— Graduates; PG— Post Graduates

TOOL OF THE STUDY

A research tool is a tool which has reliability and validity. It is used for the purpose of data collection. Reliability is the degree of consistency that the instrument or procedure demonstrates. Validity is that quality of data gathering instrument or procedure which enables it to measure what it is supposed to measure.

A research tool plays a major role in any worthwhile research, as it is the sole factor in determining sound data and in arriving at perfect conclusions about the problem or study in hand, which ultimately helps in providing suitable remedial measures to the problem concerned. The selection and use of tool can be done in two ways. The first one is to construct a tool independently by the researcher and the second one is to select a standardised tool that is already available in the field of study after assessing its suitability to the study under study.

The tool used in the present study is "Stress Questionnaire" developed by Lath Satish as it meets the research requirements of the present study.

Administration of the Tool

The tool was administered personally by the researcher on the student teachers and the sample was asked to be responded to the statements. Before giving the tool to the participants, the researcher explained the purpose of present investigation. Directions given on the cover sheet were read out to the participants and specific instructions were given. After completion the tool by the sample, they were collected to put to statistical treatment.

4

ANALYSIS OF DATA

Analysis of the data is the most skilled task of all stages of research. It depends on the judgment and skill of the researcher. It should be done by the researcher and should not be entrusted to another person. Analysis of data means studying the tabulated material in order to determine inherent facts or meanings. It involves breaking down complex factors into sample ones and putting the parts in new arrangements for the purpose of interpretation.

The first step in analysis of data is a critical examination of the assembled data. This includes the researcher to think and analyse the data in the next method of analysis, coding. Coding involves assigning symbols to each response, the purpose of which is to translate raw data into symbols. This depends upon the proper coding of responses. Coding can be done by the respondent or the observer or the interviewer. Their may be difficulties in coding due to inadequacy of data, inefficiency of the coder and lack of editing or scrutinising of the available data. Editing can be helpful for coding and for improving the quality of data collection.

Tabulation is a means of recording classification in a compact form in such a way so as to facilitate comparisons. Data is arranged in rows and columns to facilitate mathematical and statistical operations. It is of great help in the analysis and interpretation of data. While tabulating the data, the purpose of the study has to be kept in mind.

The method of analysis chosen for a particular study depends upon the nature of objectives, hypotheses to be tested, the purpose and use of the study. Statistical methods are the mathematical techniques used to facilitate the interpretation of numerical data secured from groups of individuals or group of observations or a single individual. A basic knowledge about statistics becomes inevitable for research workers, for systematic analysis and accurate and precise interpretation of data.

For the present study titled "A Study of Stress of Student Teachers", several statistical techniques were used to perform the analysis. After collecting the data from three hundred and ten student teachers through a standardised tool, the analysis was performed keeping in view the objectives framed, hypotheses formulated, data collected, tool used, etc. The highest score or lowest score one can get is 156 or 0 respectively.

For this purpose, mean, standard deviation, normal probability, critical ratio, etc., were employed.

Stress and Student Teachers

There is no stress in student teachers.

To test the validity of Hypothesis 1, the mean of the stress scores was calculated:

Table 4.1

Stress of Student Teachers

Sample	*Sample Size*	*Mean*	*Standard Deviation*
Whole	310	62.45	7.21

From the mean table of 4.1, it is evident that there was an average level of stress in student teachers.

The hypothesis that "there is no stress in student teachers" can be rejected as the student teachers are possessing an average level of stress.

Stress and Gender

There is no significant difference in the stress of male and female student teachers.

To test the validity of Hypothesis 2, the following calculations were carried out:

Table 4.2

Comparison of the Stress of Male and Female Student Teachers

Variable	*Sample Size*	*Mean*	*S.D.*	*Mean Difference*	*S.E.D.*	*C.R.*
Male	147	64.59	6.98	2.49	0.85	2.931*
Female	163	67.08	7.99			

* Significant at 0.05 level.

From the values of Table 4.2, it is evident that the stress level in male and female student teachers was significantly different, though both of them possessed an average level of stress. Female student teachers are holding more stress than their counterparts.

The hypothesis that "there is no significant difference in the stress of male and female student teachers" can be rejected as there is a significant difference in the level of stress of male and female student teachers.

Stress and Locality

There is no significant difference in the stress of rural and urban student teachers.

To test the validity of the Hypothesis 3, the following calculations were made:

Table 4.3

Comparison of the Stress of Rural and Urban Student Teachers

Variable	*Sample Size*	*Mean*	*S.D.*	*Mean Difference*	*S.E.D.*	*C.R.*
Rural	177	63.74	5.41	1.67	0.64	1.035*
Urban	133	64.41	5.82			

* Not Significant at 0.05 level.

From the values of Table 4.3, it is clear that both rural and urban student teachers were with an average level of stress, without any significant difference between them.

The hypothesis that "there is no significant difference in the stress of rural and urban student teachers" can be accepted as there is no significant difference in the level of stress of rural and urban student teachers.

Stress and Teaching Methodology

There is no significant difference in the stress of arts and science teaching methodology student teachers.

To test the validity of Hypothesis 4, the following calculations were carried out:

Table 4.4

Comparison of the Stress of Arts and Science Teaching Methodology Student Teachers

Variable	*Sample Size*	*Mean*	*S.D.*	*Mean Difference*	*SED*	*C.R.*
Arts Teachers	134	63.24	7.41	1.92	0.807	2.33*
Science Teachers	176	65.16	6.53			

* Significant at 0.05 level.

From the values of Table 4.4, it is clear that arts and science teaching methodology student teachers are with an average stress with a significant difference between them. Science student teachers are holding more stress than arts student teachers.

The hypothesis that "there is no significant difference in the stress of arts and science teaching methodology student teachers" can be rejected as there is a significant difference in the level of stress of arts and science teaching methodology student teachers.

Stress and Qualification

There is no significant difference in the stress of graduate and post-graduate student teachers.

To test the validity of Hypothesis 5, the following calculations were carried out:

Table 4.5

Comparison of the Stress of Graduate and Postgraduate Student Teachers

Variable	*Sample Size*	*Mean*	*S.D.*	*Mean Difference*	*S.E.D.*	*C.R.*
Graduates	170	67.4	7.42	1.9	0.814	2.33*
Post-graduates	140	65.5	6.89			

* Significant at 0.05 Level.

From the values of Table 4.5, it is clear that graduate and post-graduate student teachers are with an average stress with a significant difference between them. Graduate student teachers are with more stress than postgraduate student teachers.

The hypothesis that "there is no significant difference in the stress of graduate and postgraduate student teachers" can be rejected as there is a significant difference in the level of stress of graduate and postgraduate student teachers.

5

SUMMARY, CONCLUSIONS, DISCUSSION AND SUGGESTIONS

Psychologically, stress is a very important phenomenon. The term stress was first coined in 1982 by the French Mathematician Augustine Cauchy. He defined stress as a pressure per unit area. In the twentieth century, the concept of stress entered in the field of Biological Sciences. Walter Cannon (1914) conducted a psychological research which resulted in his describing the stress response as a 'fight' or 'flight' response.

Hons Selye (1936), a Canadian Endocrinologist, continued this work and devised the general adaptation syndrome, a model of how the body responds to stressful situations in the short and long term. He began the trend to describe pressures with the term 'stressors' and the biological response as 'stress'. He defined biological stress as the sum of non-specific changes in the body caused by functions or damage. Physical scientists use "stress" to indicate a force, pressure or stimulus, whereas biological scientists and psychologists use "stress" to indicate a change or response.

Stress has been defined as the state manifested by the specific syndrome, which consists of all the non-specific induced changes within a biological system.

Stress is a term used to designate non-specific body responses to any unfavourable effect. In attempting to satisfy the needs, an individual may have to face failure some times. When an individual's efforts in satisfying a need are thwarted, he is subjected to a number of stresses. Frustration, anxiety, conflicts or pressures may cause stress. A mentally healthy person will have a few occasions of stressful situations, which he will meet successfully.

The health problems may arise due to incompatibility between the demands of the educational system and the characteristics of the learner—or between learner's expectations and the educational processor both. Such incompatibilities are becoming more and more salient in the context of increasing competition in the job market, increased pressure for achievement from parents, uncertain future, and parental aspirations and their desire for compensation through their progeny.

Stress is inevitable in any educational institution. In optimal limits, it mobilises the potentialities of the students to perform more effectively. However, increasing amount of academic stress for prolonged periods may create frustration in the students which may affect their mental health, study habits and academic achievement.

Failure in examination, underachievement and the resulting stress are becoming prominent features of educational life at school as well as the higher educational levels, leading to a wide range of health problems having far-reaching consequences for individual as well as societal well-being. This is reflected in recent analyses of suicide among students.

Under these circumstances, a study has been undertaken to study the stress of student teachers pursuing B.Ed. course in the Colleges of Education of Guntur district.

The objectives of the study were:

- To find out the stress of student teachers;
- To find out the stress of male and female student teachers;
- To find out the stress of rural and urban student teachers;

- To find out the stress of arts and science teaching methodology student teachers;
- To find out the stress of graduate and post-graduate student teachers.

Variable is a condition or characteristic which the experimenter manipulates, controls or observes. For the present study the variables chosen were:

- *Gender:* Male and female student teachers;
- *Locality:* Rural and urban student teachers;
- *Teaching Methodology:* Arts and science student teachers;
- *Educational Qualifications:* Graduate and postgraduate student teachers.

Hypotheses are guesses or tentative generalisations which provide basis to the whole study. For the present study, the hypotheses framed were:

- There is no stress in student teachers;
- There is no significant difference in the stress of male and female student teachers;
- There is no significant difference in the stress of rural and urban student teachers;
- There is no significant difference in the stress of arts and science teaching methodology student teachers;
- There is no significant difference in the stress of graduate and postgraduate student teachers.

A sample is a small group which represents all the traits and characteristics of population. The student teachers studying in the Colleges of Education of Guntur district were selected as population. The stratified random sampling technique was used in selecting the sample. The sample size was 310 student teachers.

A research tool is a tool used for the purpose of data collection. The tool used in the present study was 'Stress Questionnaire' standardised by Lath Satish.

For the analysis of data, suitable statistical techniques like mean, standard deviation and critical ratio were used.

CONCLUSIONS AND DISCUSSION

From the analysis of data, the following conclusions are drawn and these are followed by necessary discussion.

The student teachers are holding an average level of stress.

The present status of stress may be due to the nature of course work as the student teachers encounter totally new content as well as new practical experiences in teaching. This may also be due to the awareness that the mastery of subject mater of pedagogy helps in getting a teacher job through the test conducted by the government, for which the student teachers need to learn and work more when compared to their previous education.

The student teachers may overcome this stress by developing better study habits, by participating in all pedagogical activities intensively, by participating in yoga, meditation, etc., by developing achievement motivation and by enhancing academic achievement. The stress can also be overcome by following relaxation techniques and mingling with co-students in performing different kinds of academic activities as per the norms and standards laid down in the course work.

The male and female student teachers are holding an average level of stress with a significant difference between them. The female teachers are with more stress than their counterparts.

The personality, mental as well as physical maturity, surrounding environment, aspirations and attitudes, etc. might have played their legitimate role in having a significant difference in the level of stress of male and female student teachers.

Both male and female student teachers should identity their position in teaching and learning arena in order to reduce their stress levels. Life skills, coping strategies and proper adjustment may help these teachers in reducing their stress levels.

The rural and urban student teachers are holding an average level of stress without any significant difference between them.

As the perspective teachers of rural and urban localities strive equally for better achievement in pedagogical activities, they should reduce the level of stress by following stress coping strategies in order to master the subject matter.

The student teachers of arts and science teaching methodologies are possessing an average level of stress with a significant difference between them. Science student teachers are with more stress than arts student teachers.

Though, both science and arts teaching methodology student teachers are having same course work in B.Ed. science students due to their cultivated sincerity might have experienced more stress than arts students. These student teachers should reduce or avoid the stress and become good teachers.

The graduate and postgraduate student teachers are with an average level of stress with a significant difference between them. The graduate student teachers are holding more stress than postgraduate student teachers.

Though, both graduate and postgraduate students are having same course work in B.Ed., due to lack of experience in professional courses, graduate students experienced more stress than post-graduate students.

The graduate and postgraduate student teachers should minimise the level of stress that appears in any kind of activity and education so that they can prove as the best teachers.

The student teachers studying in Colleges at Education are with an average level of stress. Except locality, the gender, the teaching methodology and the educational qualification of Student teachers show their influence on the level of stress of student teachers.

The student teachers, the teacher educators and the social and educational environment should make the student teachers feel comfortable during their course period. The student teachers should identify the reasons for stress and should attend to those problems by which they can avoid or at least minimise the level of stress.

Better skills, good relations with peers and teachers will help the student teachers in solving the problem of stress. Relaxation techniques, coping strategies, yoga and meditation, better study habits, good life skills, appropriate aspirations etc., may also help in reducing the stress levels of student teachers. The student teachers should avoid stress in order to master the teacher education skills and knowledge and to become expert teachers in future after rolling out of the Colleges of Education.

SUGGESTIONS FOR FURTHER RESEARCH

The present study "A Study of Stress of Student teachers", brings to light a good number of new areas to be studied by the future researchers:

1. The areas and variables that are not covered by this study may be put to test to enlighten the stress causing situations in other studies;
2. The study can be extended to students of all secondary school classes, intermediate, graduation and post graduation at district and state level;
3. Researches can be taken up to know the affect of factors like age, stage of education, socio-economic status, attitude, adjustment, creativity and other personality factors on stress;
4. Studies can be taken up to know the influence of stress on examination and achievement;
5. Studies can be considered to know the impact of education, employment, economic status, etc., of parents on the stress of children/students;
6. Studies can be undertaken to find out the influence of school environment, teachers and co-students on the stress of students.

BIBLIOGRAPHY

Aggarwal, J.C. (1994). *Essentials of Educational Psychology*. New Delhi: Vikas Publishing House Pvt. Ltd.

Buch, M.B., Chief Editor (1988). *Fourth Survey of Education Research, (1983-88)*, Volume 1. New Delhi: NCERT.

Buch, M.B., Chief Editor (1988). *Fourth Survey of Educational Research, (1983-88)*, Volume II. New Delhi: NCERT.

Buch, M.B., Chief Editor (1992). *Fifth Survey of Educational Research (1988-92)*, Volume I. New Delhi: NCERT.

Best, J.W. (1982). *Research in Education* (4th Edition). New Delhi: Prentice-Hall of India Pvt. Ltd.

Bhatiya and Bhatiya (1996). *A Text Book of Educational Psychology*. New Delhi: Doaba House.

Bhatiya, H.R. (1977). *A Text Book of Educational Psychology*. New Delhi: MacMillan India Ltd.

Chaube, S.P. (1983). *Educational Psychology*. Agra: Prints man.

Chauhan, S.S. (1978). *Advanced Educational Psychology*. New Delhi: Vikas Publishing House.

Chauhan, S.S. *Mental Hygiene—A Science of Adjustment, 2nd Edition*. New Delhi: Allied Publishers Pvt. Ltd.

Crow, L.D. and Crow, A (1991). *Educational Psychology*. New Delhi: Eurasia Publishing House Pvt. Ltd.

Dandapani, S. (February 2003). *Stress and Mental Health*. Hyderabad: EduTracks.

Das, J.P. *Text Book of Psychology*. Canada: University of Alberla Edunton.

Dosajh, N.L. (1982). *Advanced Educational Psychology*. New Delhi: Allied Publishers Pvt. Ltd.

Garret, M.E. *Statistics in Psychology and Education*. Hyderabad: International Book Bureau.

Kumar (1992). *Abnormal Psychology*. Agra: Lakshminarayan Agarwal.

Kuppu, Swami (2003). *Advanced Educational Psychology*. New Delhi: Sterling Publishers Pvt. Ltd.

Lokesh, Koul (1984). *Methodology of Educational Research*. New Delhi: Vikas Publishing House Pvt. Ltd.

Mangal, S.K. (1989). *Abnormal Psychology*. New Delhi: Sterling Publishers Pvt. Ltd.

Mangal, S.K. (2004). *Statistics in Education and Psychology*. 2nd Edition. New Delhi: Prentice-Hall of India Pvt. Ltd.

Mangal, S.K. (1998). *Psychological Foundations of Education*. Ludhiana: Prakash Brothers.

Murthy, S.K. (1983). *Essentials of Educational Psychology*. Ludhiana: Prakash Brothers.

Ramana, Bhatia (August, 2001). *Stress Management for Students*. Journal of Indian Education.

Rao, V.N. and Partha Saradhy, R. (December, 2001). *Teachers Stress*. Educational Review.

Robert, A. Baron. (1996). *Psychology*, 3rd Edition. New Delhi: Prentice-Hall of India Pvt. Ltd.

Rouald, E, Smith, Irwin, G. Sarason. *Psychology, 3rd Edition*. New York: Herper & Row Publishers.

Safaya, R.N. and Bhatia, B.D. *Educational Psychology and Guidance.* New Delhi: Dhanpat Rai and Sons.

Sharma, R.N. (1966). *Essentials of Abnormal Psychology*. Agra: Oriental Publishing House.

Sidhu, K.S. (1999). *Methodology of Research in Education*. New Delhi: Sterling Publishers Pvt. Ltd.

Vimala, T.D., Prasad Babu, B., and Bhaskara Rao, D. (2007). *Stress, Coping and Management*. New Delhi: Sonali Publications. ISBN 81-8411-086-3.

Yakaiah, P., and Bhatiya, K.K. (2003). *Introduction to Educational Psychology*. New Delhi: Kalyani Publications.

Additional References

Bhaskara Rao, Digumarti (1994). *Scientific Aptitude.* New Delhi: Ashish Publishing House. ISBN 81-7024-658-X.

Bhaskara Rao, Digumarti (1995). *Animal Kingdom.* New Delhi: Discovery Publishing House. ISBN 81-7141-274-2.

Bhaskara Rao, Digumarti (1995). *Batracology.* New Delhi: Discovery Publishing House. ISBN 81-7141-279-3.

Bhaskara Rao, Digumarti (1997). *Scientific Attitude.* New Delhi: Discovery Publishing House. ISBN 81-7141-381-1.

Bhaskara Rao, Digumarti (1996). *Scientific Attitude vis-à-vis Scientific Aptitude.* New Delhi: Discovery Publishing House. ISBN 81-7141-308-0.

Bhaskara Rao, Digumarti (2004). *Scientific Attitude, Scientific Aptitude and Achievement.* New Delhi: Discovery Publishing House. ISBN 81-7141-781-7.

Bhaskara Rao, Digumarti (2004). *Educational Administration.* New Delhi: Discovery Publishing House. ISBN 81-7141-842-2.

Bhaskara Rao, Digumarti (2004). *Issues in School Education.* New Delhi: Discovery Publishing House. ISBN 81-8356-025-3.

Bhaskara Rao, Digumarti, Editor (1996). *Encyclopaedia of Education For All,* 5 Volumes. New Delhi: APH Publishing Corporation. ISBN 81-7024-759-4 (set).

Vol. I *Education For All: The World Conference.* ISBN 81-7024-760-8.

Vol. II *Education For All: The EPA-9 Summit.* ISBN 81-7024-761-6.

Vol. III *Education For All: Quality Education For All.* ISBN 81-7024-762-6.

Vol. IV: *Education For All: Planning and Monitoring.* ISBN 81-7024-763-4.

Vol. V: *Education For All: The Indian Scenario.* ISBN 81-7024-764-0.

Bhaskara Rao, Digumarti, Editor (1996). *National Policy on Education,* 2 Volumes. New Delhi: Anmol Publications Pvt. Ltd. ISBN 81-7488-323-1.

Bhaskara Rao, Digumarti, Editor (1996). *Global Perceptions on Peace Education,* 3 Volumes. New Delhi: Discovery Publishing House. ISBN 81-7141-319-6.

Bhaskara Rao, Digumarti, Editor (1997). *Education for the 21st Century.* New Delhi: Discovery Publishing House. ISBN 81-7141-389-7.

Bhaskara Rao, Digumarti, Editor (1997). *Reflections on Scientific Attitude.* New Delhi: Discovery Publishing House. ISBN 81-7141-319-6.

Bhaskara Rao, Digumarti, Editor (1997). *Success Story of a Primary Education Project.* New Delhi: APH Publishing Corporation. ISBN 81-7024-850-7.

Bhaskara Rao, Digumarti, Editor (1997). *World Food Summit.* New Delhi: Discovery Publishing House. ISBN 81-7141-386-2.

Bhaskara Rao, Digumarti, Editor (1997). *Care the Child,* 2 Volumes. New Delhi: Discovery Publishing House. ISBN 81-7141-394-3.

Bhaskara Rao, Digumarti, Editor (1998). *Earth Summit,* 2 Volumes. New Delhi: Discovery Publishing House. ISBN 81-7141-435-4.

Bhaskara Rao, Digumarti, Editor (1998). *Adolescence Education.* New Delhi: Discovery Publishing House. ISBN 81-7141-432-X.

Bhaskara Rao, Digumarti, Editor (1998). *Community and School Nutrition Education.* New Delhi: Discovery Publishing House. ISBN 81-7141-435-4.

Bhaskara Rao, Digumarti, Editor (1998). *District Primary Education Programme.* New Delhi: Discovery Publishing House. ISBN 81-7141-396-X.

Bhaskara Rao, Digumarti, Editor (1998). *National Policy on Education: Towards an Enlightened and Humane Society.* New Delhi: Discovery Publishing House. ISBN 81-7141-426-5.

Bhaskara Rao, Digumarti, Editor (1998). *Reforming School Education.* New Delhi: Discovery Publishing House. ISBN 81-7141-403-6.

Bhaskara Rao, Digumarti, Editor (1998). *Teacher Education in India.* New Delhi: Discovery Publishing House. ISBN 81-7141-406-0.

Bhaskara Rao, Digumarti, Editor (1998). *World Summit for Social Development.* New Delhi: Discovery Publishing House. ISBN 81-7141-420-6.

Bhaskara Rao, Digumarti, Editor (1999). *International Encyclopaedia of AIDS,* 11 Volumes. New Delhi: Discovery Publishing House. ISBN 81-7141-522-6 (set).

Vol. 1 *Introduction to HIV/AIDS.* ISBN 81-7141-523-7.

Vol. 2 *HIV/AIDS—Issues and Challenges,* 2 Parts. ISBN 81-7141-524-5.

Vol. 3 *HIV/AIDS—Socio-economic Realities.* ISBN 81-7141-524-3

Vol. 4 *HIV/AIDS—Law Ethics and Human Rights,* 2 Parts. ISBN 81-7141-526-1.

Vol. 5 *AIDS and NGOs.* ISBN 81-7141-527-X.

Vol. 6 *AIDS and Home Care.* ISBN 81-7141-528-8.

Vol. 7 *STD Case Management.* ISBN 81-7141-529-6.

Vol. 8 *HIV/AIDS Prevention and Care – Teaching Modules for Nurses and Midwives.* ISBN 81-7141-530-X.

Vol. 9 *HIV Prevention Education for Educational Institutions.* ISBN 81-7141-531-8.

Vol 10 *Instructional Modules for AIDS Education.* ISBN 81-7141-532-6.

Vol.11 *School Health Education to Prevent AIDS and STD—A Package for Curriculum Planners.* ISBN 81-7141-533-4.

Bhaskara Rao, Digumarti, Editor (2000). *International Encyclopaedia of Human Rights,* 7 Volumes in 13 Parts. New Delhi: Discovery Publishing House. ISBN 81-7141-567-9 (set).

Vol. 1 *International Instruments of Human Rights,* 2 Parts. ISBN 81-7141-569-4.

Vol. 2 *Regional Instruments of Human Rights.* ISBN 81-7141-604-7.

Vol. 3 *Human Rights and the United Nations,* 2 Parts. ISBN 81-7141-605-5.

Vol. 4 Fact Files of Human Rights, 3 Parts. ISBN 81-7141-606-3.

Vol. 5 *Study Stories of Human Rights,* 3 Parts. ISBN 81-7141-607-3.

Vol. 6 *International Meetings on Human Rights,* 2 Parts. ISBN 81-714-608-X.

Vol. 7 *Professional Training in Human Rights.* ISBN 81-7141-609-8.

Bhaskara Rao, Digumarti, Editor (2000). *International Encyclopaedia of Science and Technology Education,* 11 Volumes. New Delhi: Discovery Publishing House. ISBN 81-7141-548-2 (set).

Vol.1 *Science and Technology Education.* ISBN 81-7141-568-7.

Vol. 2 *Science Education in Developing Countries.* ISBN 81-7141-569-9.

Vol.3 *Organisational Structure of Science.* ISBN 81-7141-570-9.

Vol. 4 *Science Education in Asia and the Pacific.* ISBN 81-7141-571-7

Vol. 5 *Science and Technology Education For All.* ISBN 81-7141-572-5.

Vol. 6 *Values, Ethics, Talent and Girls in Science and Technology Education.* ISBN 81-7141-573-3.

Vol. 7 *Popularization of Science and Technology Education.* ISBN 81-7141-574-1.

Vol. 8 *Science, Power and Society.* ISBN 81-7141-575-X.

Vol. 9 *Information Technology.* ISBN 81-7141-576-8.

Vol.10 *Teacher Training in Science and Technology Education.* ISBN 81-7141-577-6.

Vol. 11 *Teacher Training in Science and Technology: A Curriculum Framework.* ISBN 81-7141-578-4.

Bhaskara Rao, Digumarti, Editor (2000). *Education For All: Achieving the Goal,* 3 Volumes. New Delhi: APH Publishing Corporation. ISBN 81-7648-152-1 (set).

Vol. I *The Global Consensus.* ISBN 81-7648-155-6.

Vol. II *Mid-Decade Review Reports of Regional Seminars.* ISBN 81-7648-154-8.

Vol. III *Issues and Trends.* ISBN 81-7648-155-6.

Bhaskara Rao, Digumarti, Editor (2001). *Nuclear Materials: Issues and Concerns,* 2 Volumes. New Delhi: Discovery Publishing House. ISBN 81-7141-611-X.

Bhaskara Rao, Digumarti, Editor (2001). *Distance Education in Different Countries.* New Delhi: APH Publishing Corporation. ISBN 81-7648-229-3.

Bhaskara Rao, Digumarti, Editor (2001). *Decentralised Management of Education: Management of Education in Panchayati Raj and Municipal Bodies.* New Delhi: Discovery Publishing House. ISBN 81-7141-617-9.

Bhaskara Rao, Digumarti, Editor (2001). *Electrochemistry for Environmental Protection.* New Delhi: Discovery Publishing House. ISBN 81-7141-619-5.

Bhaskara Rao, Digumarti, Editor (2001). *Global Educational Studies.* New Delhi: Discovery Publishing House. ISBN 81-7141-616-0.

Bhaskara Rao, Digumarti, Editor (2001). *Global Synthesis of Educational Assessment.* New Delhi: Discovery Publishing House. ISBN 81-7141-613-6.

Bhaskara Rao, Digumarti, Editor (2001). *Jomtein Decade of Education*. New Delhi: Discovery Publishing House. ISBN 81-7141-618-7.

Bhaskara Rao, Digumarti, Editor (2001). *World Conference on Education for All*. New Delhi: Discovery Publishing House. ISBN 81-7141-274-9.

Bhaskara Rao, Digumarti, Editor (2001). *World Conference on Higher Education*. New Delhi: Discovery Publishing House. ISBN 81-7141-610-1.

Bhaskara Rao, Digumarti, Editor (2001). *World Conference on Science*. New Delhi: Discovery Publishing House. ISBN 81-7141-612-8.

Bhaskara Rao, Digumarti, Editor (2003). *Inspiring Experiences in Teacher Education*. New Delhi: Discovery Publishing House. ISBN 81-7141-656-X.

Bhaskara Rao, Digumarti, Editor (2003). *International Studies in Education*, 3 Volumes. New Delhi: Discovery Publishing House. ISBN 81-7141-647-0.

Bhaskara Rao, Digumarti, Editor (2003). *Military Conversion: Impact on Science and Technology*. New Delhi: Discovery Publishing House. ISBN 81-7141-578-4.

Bhaskara Rao, Digumarti, Editor (2003). *United Nations Millennium Summit*. New Delhi: Discovery Publishing House. ISBN 81-7141-632-2.

Bhaskara Rao, Digumarti, Editor (2003). *World Assembly on Aging*. New Delhi: Discovery Publishing House. ISBN 81-7141-637-3.

Bhaskara Rao, Digumarti, Editor (2003). *World Conference on Human Rights*. New Delhi: Discovery Publishing House. ISBN 81-7141-661-6.

Bhaskara Rao, Digumarti, Editor (2003). *World Education Forum*. New Delhi: Discovery Publishing House. ISBN 81-7141-639-X.

Bhaskara Rao, Digumarti, Editor (2003). *Education, Employment and Human Resource Development*. New Delhi: Discovery Publishing House. ISBN 81-7141-681-0.

Bhaskara Rao, Digumarti, Editor (2003). *Successful Schooling*. New Delhi: Discovery Publishing House. ISBN 81-7141-677-2.

Bhaskara Rao, Digumarti, Editor (2003). *European Education and Teachers.* New Delhi: Discovery Publishing House. ISBN 81-7141-702-7.

Bhaskara Rao, Digumarti, Editor (2003). *Teachers in a Changing World.* New Delhi: Discovery Publishing House. ISBN 81-7141-694-2.

Bhaskara Rao, Digumarti, Editor (2004). *International Guidelines on Open and Distance Teacher Education.* New Delhi: Discovery Publishing House. ISBN 81-7141-777-9.

Bhaskara Rao, Digumarti, Editor (2004). *Adult Learning in the 21st Century.* New Delhi: Discovery Publishing House. ISBN 81-7141-797-3.

Bhaskara Rao, Digumarti, Editor (2004). *Educational Practices: Research and Recommendations.* New Delhi: Discovery Publishing House. ISBN 81-7141-835-X.

Bhaskara Rao, Digumarti, Editor (2004). *General Secondary Education In the 21st Century.* New Delhi: Discovery Publishing House.

Bhaskara Rao, Digumarti, Editor (2004). *International Encyclopaedia of Learning to Live Together,* 4 Volumes. New Delhi: Discovery Publishing House. ISBN 81-7141-848-1.

Vol. 1 *International Conference on Learning to Live Together.*

Vol. 2 Globalisation and Living Together.

Vol. 3 *Curriculum for Learning to Live Together.*

Vol. 4 *Science Education for the Contemporary Society.*

Bhaskara Rao, Digumarti, Editor (2004). *Reforming Secondary Education.* New Delhi: Discovery Publishing House. ISBN 81-7141-843-0.

Bhaskara Rao, Digumarti, Editor (2004). *Human Rights Education.* New Delhi: Discovery Publishing House. ISBN 81-7141-882-1.

Bhaskara Rao, Digumarti, Editor (2004). *United Nations Decade for Human Rights Education.* New Delhi: Discovery Publishing House. ISBN 81-7141-887-2.

Bhaskara Rao, Digumarti, Editor (2004). *Technical and Vocational Education and Training in the 21st Century*. New Delhi: Discovery Publishing House. ISBN 81-7141-984-4.

Bhaskara Rao, Digumarti, Editor (2005). *Encyclopaedia of Education For All*, 5 Volumes. New Delhi: Discovery Publishing House.

Bhaskara Rao, Digumarti and B.S.V. Dutt, Editors (2003). *Education: Programmes and Policies*. New Delhi: APH Publishing Corporation. ISBN 81-7648-470-9.

Bhaskara Rao, Digumarti, C.A.P. Swamy and B.S.V. Dutt (1997). *Self-Evaluation in Student Teaching*. New Delhi: Discovery Publishing House. ISBN 81-7141-374-9.

Bhaskara Rao, Digumarti and D. Naresh Kumar (2004). *School Teacher Effectiveness*. New Delhi: Discovery Publishing House. ISBN 81-7141-782-5.

Bhaskara Rao, Digumarti and D. Sridhar (2002). *Job Satisfaction of School Teachers*. New Delhi: Discovery Publishing House. ISBN 81-7141-652-7.

Bhaskara Rao, Digumarti, C. Sridevi and K. Vijaya (1995). *Achievement in Social Studies*. New Delhi: Discovery Publishing House. ISBN 81-7141-281-5.

Bhaskara Rao, Digumarti and Digumarti Pushpa Latha (1994). *Achievement in Biology*. New Delhi: Discovery Publishing House. ISBN 81-7141-264-5.

Bhaskara Rao, Digumarti and Digumarti Pushpa Latha (1995). *Achievement in English*. New Delhi: Discovery Publishing House. ISBN 81-7141-283-1.

Bhaskara Rao, Digumarti and Digumarti Pushpa Latha (1994). *Achievement in Science*. New Delhi: Discovery Publishing House. ISBN 81-7141-280-70.

Bhaskara Rao, Digumarti and Digumarti Pushpa Latha (1995). *Achievement in Mathematics*. New Delhi: Discovery Publishing House. ISBN 81-7141-278-5.

Bhaskara Rao, Digumarti and Digumarti Pushpa Latha (2004). *Education for Women*. New Delhi: Discovery Publishing House. ISBN 81-7141-873-2.

Bhaskara Rao, Digumarti, Digumarti Pushpa Latha and Digumarthi Harshitha, Editors (2001). *Biological Warfare.* New Delhi: Discovery Publishing House. ISBN 81-7141-597-0.

Bhaskara Rao, Digumarti, Digumarti Pushpa Latha and Digumarthi Harshitha, Editors (2001). *Women as Educators.* New Delhi: Discovery Publishing House. ISBN 81-7141-602-0.

Bhaskara Rao, Digumarti and Digumarthi Harshitha (2004). *Adjustment of Adolescents.* New Delhi: APH Publishing House. ISBN 81-7648-836-8.

Bhaskara Rao, Digumarti and Digumarthi Harshitha, Editors (2001). *Education in India.* New Delhi: APH Publishing House. ISBN 81-7648-207-2.

Bhaskara Rao, Digumarti and Digumarti Pushpa Latha, Editors (1998). *International Encyclopaedia of Women,* 5 Volumes. New Delhi: Discovery Publishing House. ISBN 81-7141-410-9 (set).

Vol. 1 *Status of World's Women.* ISBN 81-7141-494-X.

Vol. 2 *Women, Education and Empowerment.* ISBN 81-7141-498-1.

Vol. 3 *Women Challenges and Advancement.* ISBN 81-7141-497-4.

Vol. 4 *Women and Family Health.* ISBN 81-7141-497-4.

Vol. 5 *Women and International Action.* ISBN 81-7141-498-2.

Bhaskara Rao, Digumarti, Digumarti Pushpa Latha and Digumarthi Harshitha, Editors (2001). *Assessing Learning Achievement.* New Delhi: Discovery Publishing House. ISBN 81-7141-601-2.

Bhaskara Rao, Digumarti, Digumarti Pushpa Latha and Digumarthi Harshitha, Editors (2001). *Energy Security.* New Delhi: Discovery Publishing House. ISBN 81-7141-598-9.

Bhaskara Rao, Digumarti, Digumarthi Harshitha and K.R.S. Sambasiva Rao, Editors (1999). *Advanced Biotechnology.* New Delhi: Discovery Publishing House. ISBN 81-7141-516-4.

Bhaskara Rao, Digumarti and K.R.S. Sambasiva Rao, Editors (1996). *Current Trends in Indian Education.* New Delhi: Discovery Publishing House. ISBN 81-7141-311-0.

Bhaskara Rao, Digumarti and E. Sreekanth Babu (2004). *Educational Interests of School Students*. New Delhi: Discovery Publishing House. ISBN 81-7141-837-6.

Bhaskara Rao, Digumarti and K. Vijaya (1995). *A Text Book Evaluation*. Ambala Cantt: The Associated Publishers.

Bhaskara Rao, Digumarti and M.A. Fayaz (2004). *Problems of Primary School Drop-outs*. New Delhi: Discovery Publishing House. ISBN 81-7141- 834-1.

Bhaskara Rao, Digumarti and N.V.M. Mohana Rao (2002). *Problems of Mentally Handicapped Children*. New Delhi: Discovery Publishing House. ISBN 81-7141-645-4.

Bhaskara Rao, Digumarti and S. Chandra Mohan (2002). *Sports Management*. New Delhi: APH Publishing House. ISBN 81-7648-467-9.

Bhaskara Rao, Digumarti and S.A. Khader (2004). *Problems of Private School Teachers*. New Delhi: Discovery Publishing House. ISBN 81-7141-838-4.

Bhaskara Rao, Digumarti and S.A. Khader (2004). *School Education in India*. New Delhi: Discovery Publishing Corporation. ISBN 81-7141-849-X.

Bhaskara Rao, Digumarti and Sk. Johni Basha (2004). *Teachers' Population Education Awareness*. New Delhi: Discovery Publishing House. ISBN 81-7141-832-5.

Bhaskara Rao, Digumarti, V.V. Rao, V.V. Lakshmi and V.V. Krishna, Editors (1999). *Status and Advancement of Women*. New Delhi: APH Publishing Corporation. ISBN 81-7648-169-6.

Appala Naidu, P.Ch., Author and Digumarti Bhaskara Rao, Editor (2007). *Feedback Methods and Student Performance*. New Delhi: Discovery Publishing House. ISBN 81-8356-284-1.

Babu, P.C., Author and Digumarti Bhaskara Rao, Editor (2004). *Flowers of Wisdom*. New Delhi: Discovery Publishing House. ISBN 81-7141-695-0.

Bujji Babu, K., Author and Digumarti Bhaskara Rao, Editor (2007). *Teaching Aptitude of Primary School Teachers*. New Delhi: Sonali Publications. ISBN 81-8411-083-9.

Amala, P.A. and Anupama, P., Authors and Digumarti Bhaskara Rao, Editor (2004). *History of Education.* New Delhi: Discovery Publishing House. ISBN 81-7141-860-0.

Bhagya Lakshmi, L., Author and Digumarti Bhaskara Rao, Editor (2000). *Reading and Comprehension.* New Delhi: Discovery Publishing House. ISBN 81-7141-543-1.

Bhasha, S.A., Author and Digumarti Bhaskara Rao, Editor (2004). *Methods of Teaching Geography.* New Delhi: Discovery Publishing House. ISBN 81-7141-807-4.

Bhuvaneswara Lakshmi, Gadde, Author and Digumarti Bhaskara Rao, Editor(2000). *Attitude Towards Science.* New Delhi: Discovery Publishing House. ISBN 81-7141-541-6.

Bhuvaneswara Lakshmi, G., Author and Digumarti Bhaskara Rao, Editor (2004). *Methods of Teaching Life Science.* New Delhi: Discovery Publishing House. ISBN 81-7141-804-X.

Bhuvaneswara Lakshmi, G. and K. Subba Rao, Authors and Digumarti Bhaskara Rao, Editor (2004). *Methods of Teaching Biology.* New Delhi: Discovery Publishing House. ISBN 81-7141-914-3.

Bramhaiah, T., Author and Digumarti Bhaskara Rao, Editor (2009). *Stress of Student Teachers.* New Delhi: Discovery Publishing House Pvt. Ltd.

Chary, K.V.N.B., Author and Digumarti Bhaskara Rao, Editor (2006). *Techniques of Teaching Physics.* New Delhi: Sonali Publications. ISBN 81-8411-046-4.

Chowdary, S.B.J.R. and Naga Raju, Authors and Digumarti Bhaskara Rao, Editor (2004). *Mastery of Teaching Skills.* New Delhi: Discovery Publishing House. ISBN 81-7141-861-9.

Dayakara Reddy, V. and Digumarti Bhaskara Rao, Editors (2006). *Value-Oriented Education.* New Delhi: Discovery Publishing House. ISBN 81-8356-051-2.

Devraj, T.A.S., Author and Digumarti Bhaskara Rao, Editor (1997). *Trace Analysis of Uranium and Thorium.* New Delhi: Discovery Publishing House. ISBN 81-7141-375-7.

Durga Rani, K., Author and Digumarti Bhaskara Rao, Editor (2000). *Educational Aspirations and Scientific Attitudes.* New Delhi: Discovery Publishing House. ISBN 81-7141-555-5.

Dutt, B.S.V. and Digumarti Bhaskara Rao (2001). *Empowering Primary Teachers.* New Delhi: Discovery Publishing House. ISBN 81-7141-615-2.

Dutt, B.S.V., Author and Digumarti Bhaskara Rao, editor (2004). *Comparative Education.* New Delhi: Discovery Publishing House. ISBN 81-7141-912-7.

Ediger, Marlow and Digumarti Bhaskara Rao (1996). *Science Curriculum.* New Delhi: Discovery Publishing House. ISBN 81-7141-321-8.

Ediger, Marlow and Digumarti Bhaskara Rao (2000). *Teaching Mathematics Successfully.* New Delhi: Discovery Publishing House. ISBN 81-7141-552-0.

Ediger, Marlow and Digumarti Bhaskara Rao (2001). *Teaching Science Successfully.* New Delhi: Discovery Publishing House. ISBN 81-7141-600-4.

Ediger, Marlow and Digumarti Bhaskara Rao (2001). *Teaching Social Studies Successfully.* New Delhi: Discovery Publishing House. ISBN 81-7141-596-2.

Ediger, Marlow and Digumarti Bhaskara Rao (2002). *Philosophy and Curriculum.* New Delhi: Discovery Publishing House. ISBN 81-7141-631-4.

Ediger, Marlow and Digumarti Bhaskara Rao (2002). *Improving School Administration.* New Delhi: Discovery Publishing House. ISBN 81-7141-633-0.

Ediger, Marlow and Digumarti Bhaskara Rao (2002). *Elementary Curriculum.* New Delhi: Discovery Publishing House. ISBN 81-7141-658-6.

Ediger, Marlow and Digumarti Bhaskara Rao (2003). *Language Arts Curriculum.* New Delhi: Discovery Publishing House. ISBN 81-7141-657-8.

Ediger, Marlow and Digumarti Bhaskara Rao (2003). *Psychology and Curriculum.* New Delhi: Discovery Publishing House. ISBN 81-7141-691-8.

Ediger, Marlow and Digumarti Bhaskara Rao (2003). *Teaching Language Arts Successfully*. New Delhi: Discovery Publishing House. ISBN 81-7141-678-0.

Ediger, Marlow and Digumarti Bhaskara Rao (2003). *School Curriculum and Administration*. New Delhi: Discovery Publishing House. ISBN 81-7141-709-4.

Ediger, Marlow and Digumarti Bhaskara Rao (2003). *Teaching Mathematics in Elementary Schools*. New Delhi: Discovery Publishing House. ISBN 81-7141-687-X.

Ediger, Marlow and Digumarti Bhaskara Rao (2003). *Teaching Science in Elementary Schools*. New Delhi: Discovery Publishing House. ISBN 81-7141-698-5.

Ediger, Marlow and Digumarti Bhaskara Rao (2003). *School Curriculum and Administration*. New Delhi: Discovery Publishing House. ISBN 81-7141-709-4.

Ediger, Marlow and Digumarti Bhaskara Rao (2003). *Elementary Curriculum Improvement*. New Delhi: Discovery Publishing House. ISBN 81-7141-740-X.

Ediger, Marlow and Digumarti Bhaskara Rao (2004). *School Organisation*. New Delhi: Discovery Publishing House. ISBN 81-7141-843-0.

Ediger, Marlow and Digumarti Bhaskara Rao (2004). *Relevancy in Elementary Curriculum*. New Delhi: Discovery Publishing House. ISBN 81-7141-845-9.

Ediger, Marlow and Digumarti Bhaskara Rao (2005). *Quality School Education*. New Delhi: Discovery Publishing House. ISBN 81-8356-022-9.

Ediger, Marlow and Digumarti Bhaskara Rao (2006). *Successful School Education*. New Delhi: Discovery Publishing House. ISBN 81-8356-054-7.

Ediger, Marlow and Digumarti Bhaskara Rao (2006). *Successful School Administration*. New Delhi: Discovery Publishing House. ISBN 81-8356-046-6.

Ediger, Marlow and Digumarti Bhaskara Rao (2006). *Issues in School Curriculum*. New Delhi: Discovery Publishing House. ISBN 81-8356-052-0.

Ediger, Marlow and Digumarti Bhaskara Rao (2006). *Community College—Curriculum and Teaching*. New Delhi: Discovery Publishing House. ISBN 81-8356-053-9.

Ediger, Marlow and Digumarti Bhaskara Rao (2006). *Administration of Schools*. New Delhi: Discovery Publishing House. ISBN 81-8356-244-2.

Ediger, Marlow and Digumarti Bhaskara Rao (2006). *Reading Curriculum and Instruction*. New Delhi: Discovery Publishing House. ISBN 81-8356-266-3.

Ediger, Marlow and Digumarti Bhaskara Rao (2006). *Curriculum Organisation*. New Delhi: Discovery Publishing House. ISBN 81-8356-205-1.

Ediger, Marlow and Digumarti Bhaskara Rao (2006). *Curriculum of School Subjects*. New Delhi: Discovery Publishing House. ISBN 81-8356-207-8.

Ediger, Marlow, B.S.V. Dutt and Digumarti Bhaskara Rao (2003). *Teaching English Successfully*. New Delhi: Discovery Publishing House. ISBN 81-7141-707-8.

Ediger, Marlow and Digumarti Bhaskara Rao (2007). *School Science Education*. New Delhi: Discovery Publishing House. ISBN 81-8356-352-X.

Ediger, Marlow and Digumarti Bhaskara Rao (2007). *Language Arts Education*. New Delhi: Discovery Publishing House. ISBN 81-8356-333-3.

Elizabeth, M.E.S., Author and Digumarti Bhaskara Rao, Editor (2004). *Methods of Teaching English*. New Delhi: Discovery Publishing House. ISBN 81-7141-809-0.

Elizabeth, M.E.S., Author and Digumarti Bhaskara Rao, Editor (2004). *Acquisition of English Vocabulary*. New Delhi: Discovery Publishing House. ISBN 81-8356-075-X.

Fatima, Sk. Author and Digumarti Bhaskara Rao, Editor (2007). *Reasoning Ability of School Students.* New Delhi: Discovery Publishing House. ISBN 81-8356-330-9.

Fatima, Sk. and Digumarti Bhaskara Rao (2008). *Reasoning Ability of Adolescent Students.* New Delhi: Discovery Publishing House Pvt. Ltd. ISBN 978-81-8356-315-4.

Gopala Krishna, M., Author and Digumarti Bhaskara Rao, Editor (2007). *Techniques of Teaching Physical Education.* New Delhi: Sonali Publications. ISBN 81-8411-044-8.

Gopala Krishna, M., Author and Digumarti Bhaskara Rao, Editor (2007). *Techniques of Teaching Education.* New Delhi: Sonali Publications. ISBN 81-8411-062-6.

Harshitha, Digumarthi, Author and Digumarti Bhaskara Rao, Editor (2004). *Methods of Teaching Information Technology.* New Delhi: Discovery Publishing House. ISBN 81-7141-805-8.

Harshitha, Digumarthi, Author and Digumarti Bhaskara Rao, Editor (2007). *Techniques of Teaching Computer Science.* New Delhi: Sonali Publications. ISBN 81-8411-036-7.

Indira Devi, Author and J. Prasanth Kumar and Digumarti Bhaskara Rao, Editors (2004). *Values in Language Text Books.* New Delhi: Discovery Publishing House. ISBN 81-7141-833-3.

Jalaja Kumari, C., Author and Digumarti Bhaskara Rao, Editor (2004). *Methods of Teaching Educational Technology.* New Delhi: Discovery Publishing House. ISBN 81-7141-810-4.

Jalaja Kumari, C., Author and Digumarti Bhaskara Rao, Editor (2007). *Job Satisfaction of Teachers.* New Delhi: Discovery Publishing House. ISBN 81-8356-329-5.

Janardhan Reddy, B., Author and Digumarti Bhaskara Rao, Editor (2006). *Techniques of Teaching Sociology.* New Delhi: Sonali Publications. ISBN 81-8411-042-1.

Jayalakshmi, M., Author and Digumarti Bhaskara Rao, Editor (2008). *Microteaching and Prospective Teachers.* New Delhi: Discovery Publishing House Pvt. Ltd.

Jayasree, K., Author and Digumarti Bhaskara Rao, Editor (1999). *Correlates of Socialisation*. New Delhi: Discovery Publishing House. ISBN 81-7141-517-2.

Jayasree, K., Author and Digumarti Bhaskara Rao, Editor (2004). *Methods of Teaching Science*. New Delhi: Discovery Publishing House. ISBN 81-7141-801-5.

John Babu, C., Author and T.J.R. Prasad, G.M. Madhukar and Digumarti Bhaskara Rao, Editors (2004). *Problem Solving in Mathematics*. New Delhi: APH Publishing Corporation. ISBN 81-7648-273-0.

Joseph Raju, B and G.A. Anitha, Authors and Digumarti Bhaskara Rao, Editor (2004). *Population Education*. New Delhi: Sonali Publications. ISBN 81-88836-31-3.

Lalitha, T., Author and K.S. Prabhakaram, D.S.N. Sastry and Digumarti Bhaskara Rao, Editors (2004). *Educational Philosophic Beliefs*. New Delhi: Discovery Publishing House. ISBN 81-7141-765-5.

Krishna, G., Author and Digumarti Bhaskara Rao, Editor (2006). *Techniques of Teaching Physical Education*. New Delhi: Sonali Publications. ISBN 81-8411-044-8.

Kumar Raja, G., Author and Digumarti Bhaskara Rao, Editor (2007). *Principles of Primary School*. New Delhi: Sonali Publications. ISBN 81-8411-054-5.

Lakshmi Kumari, V., Author and Digumarti Bhaskara Rao, Editor (2006). *Techniques of Teaching Home Science*. New Delhi: Sonali Publications. ISBN 81-8411-048-0.

Madhava, K., Author and Digumarti Bhaskara Rao, Editor (2008). *Personality of Adolescent Students*. New Delhi: Sonali Publications.

Madhu Bala, Jampala, Author and Digumarti Bhaskara Rao, Editor (2004). *Methods of Teaching Exceptional Children*. New Delhi: Discovery Publishing House. ISBN 81-7141-802-3.

Madhu Bala, Jampala, Author and Digumarti Bhaskara Rao, Editor (2007). *Adjustment Problems of Hearing Impaired*. New Delhi: Discovery Publishing House. ISBN 81-7141-831-7.

Marja, Talvi and Digumarti Bhaskara Rao, Editors (1996). *Educational Leadership and Social Changes*. New Delhi: Discovery Publishing House. ISBN 81-7141-320-X.

Mohana Sundari, C., Author and B. Prasad Babu and Digumarti Bhaskara Rao, Editors (2008). *Stress Among Pregnant Women* New Delhi: Discovery Publishing House Pvt. Ltd. ISBN 978-81-8356-316-1.

Naga Kumari, U., Author and Digumarti Bhaskara Rao, Editor (2008). *Science Process Skills of School Students*. New Delhi: Discovery Publishing House Pvt. Ltd. ISBN 978-81-8356-263-8.

Nageswara Rao, S. and M. Srihari, Authors and Digumarti Bhaskara Rao, Editor (2004). *Guidance and Counselling*. New Delhi: Discovery Publishing House. ISBN 81-7141-840-6.

Nageswara Rao, S., Author and Digumarti Bhaskara Rao, Editor (2006). *Techniques of Teaching Psychology*. New Delhi: Sonali Publications. ISBN 81-8411-040-5.

Nageswara Rao, S. and P. Sridhar, Authors and Digumarti Bhaskara Rao, Editor (2004). *Methods and Techniques of Teaching*. New Delhi: Sonali Publications. ISBN 81-88836-33-8.

Nirmala Jyothi, M., Author and Digumarti Bhaskara Rao, Editor (2003). *Non-detention System in School Education*. New Delhi: Discovery Publishing House. ISBN 81-7141-654-3.

Padma Tulasi, G., Author and Digumarti Bhaskara Rao, Editor (2004). *Methods of Teaching Elementary Science*. New Delhi: Discovery Publishing House. ISBN 81-7141-871-6.

Pala Prasada Rao, V., Author and K. N. Rani and D. Bhaskara Rao, Editors (2004). *India Pakistan: Partition Perspectives in Indo English Novels*. New Delhi: Discovery Publishing House. ISBN 81-7141-871-6.

Pala Prasada Rao, V., Author and D. Bhaskara Rao, Editors (2008). *Functioning of Autonomous Colleges*. New Delhi: Discovery Publishing House Pvt. Ltd. ISBN 978-81-8356-258-4.

Pitchi Reddy, M., Author and Digumarti Bhaskara Rao, Editor (2007). *Techniques of Teaching Social Sciences*. New Delhi: Sonali Publications. ISBN 81-8411-066-X.

Prasad Babu, B., Author and P. Madhu and Digumarti Bhaskara Rao, Editors (2006). *Psychological Adjustment and Well-being*. New Delhi: Discovery Publishing House. ISBN 81-8356-204-3.

Prasad Babu, B., Author and M.V.R. Raju and Digumarti Bhaskara Rao, Editors (2006). *Behavioural Problems of School Children*. New Delhi: Discovery Publishing House. ISBN 81-8356-206-X.

Prabhakaram, K.S., Author and Digumarti Bhaskara Rao, Editors (1998). *Concept Attainment Model in Mathematics Teaching*. New Delhi: Discovery Publishing House. ISBN 81-7141-424-9.

Prasanth Kumar, J., Author and Digumarti Bhaskara Rao, Editor (1998). *Effectiveness of Distance Education System*. New Delhi: Discovery Publishing House. ISBN 81-7141-437-0.

Prasanth Kumar, J., Author and Digumarti Bhaskara Rao, Editor (2004). *Methods of Teaching Civics*. New Delhi: Discovery Publishing House. ISBN 81-7141-806-6.

Prasanth Kumar, J., Author and G. Sundara Rao and Digumarti Bhaskara Rao, Editors (2000). *Open University Student Support Services*. New Delhi: Discovery Publishing House. ISBN 81-7141-550-4.

Raja Kumari, M.A. and D.R.S. Sundari, Authors and Digumarti Bhaskara Rao, Editor (2004). *Special Education*. New Delhi: Discovery Publishing House. ISBN 81-7141-846-5.

Raja Kumari, M.A. and D.R.S. Sundari, Authors and Digumarti Bhaskara Rao, Editor (2004). *Methods of Teaching Educational Psychology*. New Delhi: Discovery Publishing House. ISBN 81-7141-820-1.

Rajeswari, S. M., Author and T. Santhanam, B. Prasad Babu and Digumarti Bhaskara Rao, Editors (2008). *Stress and Attitude of Women Teachers*. New Delhi: Discovery Publishing House Pvt. Ltd. ISBN 978-81-8356-324-6.

Ramatulasamma, K., Author and Digumarti Bhaskara Rao, Editor (2002). *Job Satisfaction of Teacher Educators*. New Delhi: Discovery Publishing House. ISBN 81-7141-655-1.

Rama Krishnaiah, D., Author and Digumarti Bhaskara Rao, Editor (1998). *Job Satisfaction of College Teachers.* New Delhi: Discovery Publishing House. ISBN 81-7141-438-9.

Rama Kumar Ratnam, M.V., Author and Digumarti Bhaskara Rao, Editor (1998). *Dukkha: Suffering in Early Buddhism.* New Delhi: Discovery Publishing House. ISBN 81-7141-653-5.

Rama Krishna Prasad and P. Vide Sagar, Authors and Digumarti Bhaskara Rao, Editor (2004). *Methods of Teaching Physical Education.* New Delhi: Discovery Publishing House. ISBN 81-7141-868-6.

Rama Seshaiah, P. Author and Digumarti Bhaskara Rao, Editor (2004). *Methods of Teaching Home Science.* New Delhi: Discovery Publishing House. ISBN 81-7141-916-X.

Rama Swamy, K., Author and Digumarti Bhaskara Rao, Editor (2007). *Techniques of Teaching Environmental Science.* New Delhi: Sonali Publications. ISBN 81-8411-035-9.

Ramesh, A.R., Author and Digumarti Bhaskara Rao, Editor (2006). *Techniques of Teaching Commerce.* New Delhi: Sonali Publications. ISBN 81-8411-043-X.

Ramesh, Ghanta and Digumarti Bhaskara Rao, Editors (1998). *Environmental Education: Problems and Prospects.* New Delhi: Discovery Publishing House. ISBN 81-7141-423-0.

Ranga Rao, B., Author and Digumarti Bhaskara Rao, Editor (2007). *Techniques of Teaching Economics.* New Delhi: Sonali Publications. ISBN 81-8411-056-1.

Ranga Rao, R., Author and Digumarti Bhaskara Rao, Editor (2004). *Methods of Teacher Teaching.* New Delhi: Discovery Publishing House. ISBN 81-7141-812-0.

Rani, S.S., Author and Digumarti Bhaskara Rao, Editor (2006). *Techniques of Teaching Botany.* New Delhi: Sonali Publications. ISBN 81-8411-037-5.

Rathaiah, Lavu and Digumarti Bhaskara Rao, Editors (1996), *International Innovations in Education.* New Delhi: Discovery Publishing House. ISBN 81-7141-359-5.

Rathaiah, Lavu and Digumarti Bhaskara Rao (1997). *Achievement Correlates*. New Delhi: Discovery Publishing House. ISBN 81-7141-385-4.

Ravi Krishna, M., Author and Digumarti Bhaskara Rao, Editor (2004). *Examination System*. New Delhi: Discovery Publishing House. ISBN 81-7141-824-4.

Ravi Kumar, M., Author and Digumarti Bhaskara Rao, Editor (2004). *Methods of Teaching Computer Science*. New Delhi: Discovery Publishing House. ISBN 81-7141-823-6.

Roja Ramani, V., Author and Digumarti Bhaskara Rao, Editor (2008). *Frustration of Student Teachers*. New Delhi: Discovery Publishing House Pvt. Ltd.

Rudramamba, B., Author and Digumarti Bhaskara Rao, Editor (2003). *Problems of Teaching*. New Delhi: APH Publishing Corporation. ISBN 81-7648-462-8.

Rudramamba, B. and V. Lakshmi Kumari, Authors and Digumarti Bhaskara Rao, Editor (2004). *Methods of Teaching Economics*. New Delhi: Discovery Publishing House. ISBN 81-7141-900-3.

Sambasiva Rao, P., Author and Digumarti Bhaskara Rao, Editor (2007). *Techniques of Teaching Psychology*. New Delhi: Sonali Publications. ISBN 81-8411-040-5.

Sanjeeva Rao, P.C., Author and Digumarti Bhaskara Rao, Editor (1996). *A Text Book of Geology*. New Delhi: Discovery Publishing House. ISBN 81-7141-313-7.

Santhanam, T., B. Prasad Babu and S. Sugandhi, Authors and Digumarti Bhaskara Rao, Editor (2007). *Children with Learning Disabilities*. New Delhi: Sonali Publications. ISBN 81-8411-077-4.

Santhanam, T., B. Prasad Babu and S. Sugandhi, Authors and Digumarti Bhaskara Rao, Editor (2008). *Learning Disabilities and Remedial Programmes*. New Delhi: Discovery Publishing House Pvt. Ltd. ISBN 978-81-8356-257-7.

Sarala, M.M.O., Author and Digumarti Bhaskara Rao, Editor (2006). *Techniques of Teaching English*. New Delhi: Sonali Publications. ISBN 81-8411-047-2.

Satya Narayana, G., Author and Digumarti Bhaskara Rao, Editor (2008). *Attitude Towards Social Studies and Achievement in Social Studies*. New Delhi: Discovery Publishing House Pvt. Ltd. ISBN 978-81-8356-261-4.

Satya Narayana, V., Author and Digumarti Bhaskara Rao, Editor (2001). *Physical Education, Social Attitudes and Leadership Qualities*. New Delhi: Discovery Publishing House. ISBN 81-7141-593-8.

Satya Narayana, P.V.V. and G. Krishna, Authors and Digumarti Bhaskara Rao, Editor (2004). *Curriculum Development and Management*. New Delhi: Discovery Publishing House. ISBN 81-7141-813-9.

Shamsuddin, Sk. and V. Dayakara Reddy, Authors and Digumarti Bhaskara Rao, Editor (2007). *Values and Academic Achievement*. New Delhi: Discovery Publishing House. ISBN 81-8356-283-3.

Singh, Y.C., Author and Digumarti Bhaskara Rao, Editor (2006). *Techniques of Teaching Science*. New Delhi: Sonali Publications. ISBN 81-8411-041-3.

Sirisha Rani, S., Author and Digumarti Bhaskara Rao, Editor (2007). *Techniques of Teaching Botany*. New Delhi: Sonali Publications. ISBN 81-8411-037-5.

Sivaratnam Reddy, M., Author and Digumarti Bhaskara Rao, Editor (2004). *Creativity in College Students*. New Delhi: Discovery Publishing House. ISBN 81-7141-697-7.

Siva Lakshmi, G.V. and G.L. Subbaiah, Authors and Digumarti Bhaskara Rao, Editor (2004). *Methods of Teaching Environmental Science*. New Delhi: Discovery Publishing House. ISBN 81-7141-839-2.

Srinivas, G. and Digumarti Bhaskara Rao (2007). *Anxiety of Student Teachers*. New Delhi: Sonali Publications. ISBN 81-8411-084-7.

Srinivas, M. and I. Prasada Rao, Authors and Digumarti Bhaskara Rao, Editor (2004). *Methods of Teaching History*. New Delhi: Discovery Publishing House. ISBN 81-7141-803-1.

Srinivas Rao, P., Author and Digumarti Bhaskara Rao, Editor (2007). *Principles of Secondary School*. New Delhi: Sonali Publications. ISBN 81-8411-058-8.

Srinivasulu Reddy, M. and K.R.S. Sambasiva Rao, Authors and Digumarti Bhaskara Rao, Editor (1999). *A Text Book of Aquaculture.* New Delhi: Discovery Publishing House. ISBN 81-7141-482-6.

Srinivasa Rao, Mandalapu, Author and Digumarti Bhaskara Rao, Editor (2003). *Achievement Motivation and Achievement in Mathematics.* New Delhi: Discovery Publishing House. ISBN 81-7141-674-8.

Srihari, M., Author and Digumarti Bhaskara Rao, Editor (2003). *Values of Prospective Teachers.* New Delhi: Discovery Publishing House. ISBN 81-8356-328-7.

Subba Rao, K., Author and Digumarti Bhaskara Rao, Editor (2007). *School Education Policy.* New Delhi: Discovery Publishing House. ISBN 81-8356-285-X.

Subba Rao, K., Author and Digumarti Bhaskara Rao, Editor (2007). *Educational Planning.* New Delhi: Sonali Publications. ISBN 81-8411-053-7.

Sudhakar Reddy, Y., Author and Digumarti Bhaskara Rao, Editor (2003). *Creativity in Adolescents.* New Delhi: Discovery Publishing House. ISBN 81-7141-659-4.

Sunil Kumar, K. and K. Rama Krishana, Authors and Digumarti Bhaskara Rao, Editor (2004). *Methods of Teaching Chemistry.* New Delhi: Discovery Publishing House. ISBN 81-7141-913-5.

Suneetha, G., Author and Digumarti Bhaskara Rao, Editor (2004). *Environmental Awareness of School Students.* New Delhi: Sonali Publications. ISBN 81-8411-085-5.

Sunita, E. and R. Sambasiva Rao, Authors and Digumarti Bhaskara Rao, Editor (2004). *Methods of Teaching Mathematics.* New Delhi: Discovery Publishing House. ISBN 81-7141-915-1.

Suresh, K., Author and Digumarti Bhaskara Rao, Editor (2008). *Social Intelligence of Student Teachers.* New Delhi: Sonali Publications.

Surya Madhava, I., Author and Digumarti Bhaskara Rao, Editor (2006). *Techniques of Teaching Geography.* New Delhi: Sonali Publications. ISBN 81-8411-034-0.

Surya Madhava, I., Author and Digumarti Bhaskara Rao, Editor (2007). *Techniques of Teaching Political Science.* New Delhi: Sonali Publications. ISBN 81-8411-061-8.

Suvarna Raju, T.J.M., Author and M.V.R. Raju, B. Prasad Babu and Digumarti Bhaskara Rao, Editors (2008). *Personality and Adjustment of University Hostel Students.* New Delhi: Sonali Publications.

Swamy, K.R., Author and Digumarti Bhaskara Rao, Editor (2006). *Techniques of Teaching Environmental Science.* New Delhi: Sonali Publications. ISBN 81-8411-035-9.

Swarna Jyothi, K., Author and Digumarti Bhaskara Rao, Editor (2007). *Educational Research.* New Delhi: Sonali Publications. ISBN 81-8411-063-4.

Swarna Latha, C.D., and Digumarti Bhaskara Rao, Editors (2006). *Encyclopaedia of Biotechnology,* 5 Volumes. New Delhi: Discovery Publishing House. ISBN 81-8356-168-3.

Swarupa Rani, T. and J.R. Priyadarshini, Authors and Digumarti Bhaskara Rao, Editor (2004). *Educational Measurement and Evaluation.* New Delhi: Discovery Publishing House. ISBN 81-7141-859-7.

Vanaja, M., Author and Digumarti Bhaskara Rao, Editor (1999). *Inquiry Training Model.* New Delhi: Discovery Publishing House. ISBN 81-7141-515-6.

Vanaja, M., Author and Digumarti Bhaskara Rao, Editor (2004). *Methods of Teaching Physics.* New Delhi: Discovery Publishing House. ISBN 81-7141-867-8.

Valeri V. Koustiouk, Author and Digumarti Bhaskara Rao, Editor (2002). *A Text Book of Cryogenics.* New Delhi: Discovery Publishing House. ISBN 81-7141-642-X.

Vamsi Krishna, V., Author and Digumarti Bhaskara Rao, Editor (2004). *School Psychology.* New Delhi: Discovery Publishing House. ISBN 81-7141-880-5.

Veena Kumari, Balusu and Digumarti Bhaskara Rao (1996). *Operation Black Board.* New Delhi: APH Publishing Corporation. ISBN 81-7024-711-X.

Veena Kumari, Balusu, Author and Digumarti Bhaskara Rao, Editor (2004). *Methods of Teaching Social Studies*. New Delhi: Discovery Publishing House. ISBN 81-7141-899-6.

Veena Kumari, Balusu, Author and Digumarti Bhaskara Rao, Editor (2000). *Psycho-Social Correlates of Achievement*. New Delhi: Discovery Publishing House. ISBN 81-7141-547-4.

Venkata Rao, B., Author and Digumarti Bhaskara Rao, Editor (2007). *Techniques of Teaching Chemistry*. New Delhi: Sonali Publications. ISBN 81-8411-057-X.

Venkata Rao, P. and Digumarti Bhaskara Rao (1989). *A Text Book of Zoology – Junior Intermediate*. Guntur: Vignan Publishers.

Venkata Rao, P. and Digumarti Bhaskara Rao (1989). *A Text Book of Zoology – Senior Intermediate*. Guntur: Vignan Publishers.

Venkateswara Rao, V., Author and Digumarti Bhaskara Rao, Editor (2004). *Problems of Education*. New Delhi: Discovery Publishing House. ISBN 81-7141-841-4.

Venkateswara Rao, V., V. Vijaya Lakshmi and V. Vamsi Krishna, Authors and Digumarti Bhaskara Rao, Editor (2004). *Education For All*. New Delhi: Sonali Publications. ISBN 81-88836-30-3.

Venkateswara Rao, V., V. Vijaya Lakshmi and V. Vamsi Krishna, Authors and Digumarti Bhaskara Rao, Editor (2004). *Education in India*. New Delhi: Sonali Publications. ISBN 81-88836-858-9.

Venkateswara Reddy, L. and Narayana, M. L., Authors and Digumarti Bhaskara Rao, Editor (2004). *Education for Dalits*. New Delhi: Discovery Publishing House. ISBN 81-7141-872-4.

Venkateswara Reddy, L. and Narayana, M.L, Authors and Digumarti Bhaskara Rao, Editor (2004). *Methods of Teaching Rural Sociology*. New Delhi: Discovery Publishing House. ISBN 81-7141-811-2.

Venkateswarlu, K. and S.J. Basha, Authors and Digumarti Bhaskara Rao, Editor (2004). *Methods of Teaching Commerce*. New Delhi: Discovery Publishing House. ISBN 81-7141-808-2.

Venugopala Rao, K., Author and Digumarti Bhaskara Rao, Editor (2000). *Teacher Morale in Secondary Schools*. New Delhi: Discovery Publishing House. ISBN 81-7141-551-2.

Venugopala Rao, K., Author and Digumarti Bhaskara Rao, Editor (2007). *Techniques of Teaching History*. New Delhi: Sonali Publications. ISBN 81-8411-059-6.

Vidya, C., Author and Digumarti Bhaskara Rao, Editor (1996). *A Text Book of Nutrition*. New Delhi: Discovery Publishing House. ISBN 81-7141-309-9.

Vimala, T.D., B. Prasad Babu and Digumarti Bhaskara Rao, Editors (2007). *Stress, Coping and Management*. New Delhi: Sonali Publications. ISBN 81-8411-086-3.

Vijaya Bharathi, D., Author and Digumarti Bhaskara Rao, Editor (2000). *Educational Philosophies of Swami Vivekananda and John Dewey*. New Delhi: APH Publishing House. ISBN 81-7648-309-9.

Vijaya Bharathi, D., Author and Digumarti Bhaskara Rao, Editor (2005). *Educational Philosophy of John Dewey*. New Delhi: Discovery Publishing House. ISBN 81-8356-024-5.

Vijaya Bharathi, D., Author and Digumarti Bhaskara Rao, Editor (2005). *Educational Philosophy of Swami Vivekananda*. New Delhi: Discovery Publishing House. ISBN 81-8356-023-7.

Vijaya Lakshmi, D., Author and Digumarti Bhaskara Rao, Editor (2004) *Basic Education*. New Delhi: Discovery Publishing House. ISBN 81-7141-881-3.

Vijaya Lakshmi, V., Author and Digumarti Bhaskara Rao, Editor (2006). *Techniques of Teaching Music*. New Delhi: Sonali Publications. ISBN 81-8411-038-3.

Vijaya Kumar, S.J., Author and Digumarti Bhaskara Rao, Editor (2006). *Techniques of Teaching Mathematics*. New Delhi: Sonali Publications. ISBN 81-8411-039-1.

Visalakshi, V., Author and Digumarti Bhaskara Rao, Editor (2006). *Techniques of Teaching Biology*. New Delhi: Sonali Publications. ISBN 81-8411-045-6.

Visalakshi, V., Author and Digumarti Bhaskara Rao, Editor (2007). *Techniques of Teaching Zoology*. New Delhi: Sonali Publications. ISBN 81-8411-055-3.

Books in Telugu Language

Bhaskara Rao, Digumarti (1986). *Dhrushya Sravana Bodhanapakaranalu* (Audio-Visual Teaching Aids). Guntur: Nagarjuna Publishers.

Bhaskara Rao, Digumarti (1993). *Jeevasasthra Bodhana* (Teaching of Biology). Guntur: Nagarjuna Publishers.

Bhaskara Rao, Digumarti (1995). *Vignanasasthra Bodhana* (Teaching of Science) Guntur: Nagarjuna Publishers.

Bhaskara Rao, Digumarti (1997). *Vidya Manovignana Sasthram* (Educational Psychology). Guntur: Creative Press.

Bhaskara Rao, Digumarti (1998). *DSC Study Material*. Guntur: Nagarjuna Publishers.

Bhaskara Rao, Digumarti (1998). *Upadhyayudu Vidya*. (Teacher and Education) Guntur: Nagarjuna Publishers.

Bhaskara Rao, Digumarti (1998). *Vidya Drukpadalu* (Perspectives of Education). Guntur: Nagarjuna Publishers.

Bhaskara Rao, Digumarti (1999). *EdCET Teaching Aptitude*. Guntur: Nagarjuna Publishers.

Bhaskara Rao, Digumarti (2001). *Bharata Samajamulo Upadyayudu Vidhya* (Teacher and Education in Emerging Indian Society). Guntur: Sri Nagarjuna Publishers.

Bhaskara Rao, Digumarti (2001). *Bhoutika Sasthra Bodhana Padhatulu* (Methods of Teaching Physical Science). Guntur: Sri Nagarjuna Publishers.

Bhaskara Rao, Digumarti (2001). *Jeeva Sasthra Bodhana Padhatulu* (Methods of Teaching Biology).Guntur: Sri Nagarjuna Publishers.

Bhaskara Rao, Digumarti (2001). *Vidya Manovignana Sasthram* (Educational Psychology). Guntur: Sri Nagarjuna Publishers.

Bhaskara Rao, Digumarti (2003). *Patasala Yajamanyam/Paripalana* (School Management and Administration). Guntur: Sri Nagarjuna Publishers.

Gopala Krishna, G., A. Rama Krishna, K. Subba Rao and Bhaskara Rao, Digumarti (2004). *Jeevasasthra Bodhana Padhatulu* (Methods of Teaching of Biological Science). Guntur: Sri Nagarjuna Publishers.

Krishna Murthy, V., K.S. Sudheer Reddy and Digumarti Bhaskara Rao (2004). *Vidya Manovignana Sasthra Adharalu* (Foundations of Educational Psychology). Guntur: Sri Nagarjuna Publishers.

Lalini, V., V. Dayakara Reddy, M. Srihari and Digumarti Bhaskara Rao (2004). *Vidya Adharalu* (Foundations of Education). Guntur: Sri Nagarjuna Publishers.

Subba Rao, K.P., P. Ayodhya and Digumarti Bhaskara Rao (2004). *Patasala Yajamanyam—Vidhya Vyavasthalu* (School Management and Systems of Education). Guntur: Sri Nagarjuna Publishers.

Sudhakar, V., B. Ravindra Babu, D.S. Kumar and Digumarti Bhaskara Rao (2004). *Vidya Sanketika Sasthram—Computer Vidhya* (Educational Technology and Computer Education). Guntur: Sri Nagarjuna Publishers.

Index

❑❑❑